THE
REGENERATIVE
KITCHEN

A **WILD PASTURES** COOKBOOK
WITH **OVER 100** DELICIOUS + SUSTAINABLE
FARM TO TABLE **RECIPES**

Wild Pastures LLC
150 Wells St. #1018
Erie, CO 80516
https://wildpastures.com

Ordering Information:
For details, contact support@wildpastures.com.

Print ISBN: 978-1-7371466-0-5

eBook ISBN: 978-1-7371466-1-2

Printed in the United States of America on SFI Certified paper.
Second Edition

TABLE OF CONTENTS

WILD PASTURES

ABOUT WILD PASTURES

NOT THE COW, BUT THE HOW

As climate change continues to be the biggest threat to our planet, a lot of people find themselves asking: What can I do to help? If you're one of these people, you're in the right place.

Wild Pastures was created to make getting truly grass fed, pasture-raised meat, raised on American farms dedicated to regenerative practices quick, easy, and affordable. By supporting the American farmers who are dedicated to these practices, you're taking a huge step in helping restore nutrient density to our soil and sequester carbon from the atmosphere back into the ground where it belongs.

Inside this cookbook you'll find over 100 recipes specifically created using regeneratively raised meat in mind. It was created for those who care about supporting American farmers. The health-conscious who care about avoiding things like hormones and antibiotics in their food. The budgeters who don't want to spend a fortune just to get high-quality meat. Parents who care about their children and their children's children having a planet to call home. People like you who understand: **It's not the cow, it's the how.**

90% of animal products you see in grocery stores come from concentrated animal feeding operations (CAFO's), better known as factory farms. These factory farms are bad for the animals, bad for the humans who eat that meat, and detrimental to the environment.

What's worse? Labeling restrictions are so vague that it can feel impossible as a consumer to know what kind of meat you're buying. Meat labeled as "grass fed" oftentimes is finished on grains. Meat labeled "Product of the U.S.A." can be labeled this way as long as it was packaged in America, meaning it was likely shipped from overseas. Plus, these labels come with much higher price tags.

That's where Wild Pastures comes in. We're able to offer near wholesale prices by cutting out the middleman and bringing you regeneratively raised meat directly from small, American farms to your kitchen table.

Regenerative agriculture focuses on healing our degraded soils with practices like crop rotation, animal integration with holistic grazing, and increased biodiversity. When dust is transformed back into soil, carbon can be sequestered, helping the environment and decreasing drought and flood risk as the soils' water holding capacity is restored.

As an added bonus, this meat is more nutritious and packed with more flavor than anything you'll get at your local grocery store. With the recipes you'll find in this cookbook, you'll have all the tools you need to create a delicious, environmentally friendly meal using your Wild Pastures chicken, beef, pork, or seafood.

We've identified which recipes work with which diets. So whether you're Keto, Paleo, gluten-free, dairy-free, or something else, you can easily identify which recipes fit with your lifestyle.

From the entire Wild Pastures team, thank you for opting out of factory farmed meat today and joining our mission to heal our planet. Enjoy!

THE CONTINUOUS COOKBOOK

ALL ABOUT QR CODES

At Wild Pastures, we never want you to be without the resources you need to enjoy all the wonderful meat and seafood we have to offer. This is why we've created the continuous cookbook!

We are always expanding our recipe collection, and want to make sure you have access to any and all recipes, even if they aren't included in this cookbook. That's why, at the bottom of each recipe, we've included a QR code. Simply scan the QR code with your phone, and you'll be redirected to all the Wild Pastures recipes that use that specific kind of meat.

If you scan the QR code on a recipe that uses boneless, skinless chicken breasts, you'll be taken to a page on our site with every recipe Wild Pastures has for boneless, skinless chicken breasts. If the recipe uses ground beef, you'll have every ground beef recipe. And so on... This way you will have access to an endless library of Wild Pastures recipes available at your fingertips! To see all of the recipes we have to offer, go ahead and scan the QR code below to head over to our Wild Pastures recipe page and start exploring. Enjoy!

**JUST SCAN THE QR CODE
WITH YOUR PHONE CAMERA!**

CHOOSING THE RIGHT RECIPE

At Wild Pastures we're dedicated to providing a variety of recipes that fit every lifestyle. That's why each recipe has dietary labels to make choosing your next meal a breeze no matter what diet you are following!

 PALEO This icon means the recipe is compliant with a Paleo diet which typically includes meat, fish, fruit and/or vegetables while avoiding refined carbs, sugar and dairy.

 KETO This icon indicates the recipe fits with the Keto diet. These recipes contain high fat, high protein and low carb ingredients.

 GLUTEN-FREE This icon indicates the recipe is gluten-free.

 DAIRY-FREE This icon indicates the recipe is dairy-free.

FAQ

WHAT DO YOU MEAN BY REGENERATIVE FARMING?

Thank you so much for asking! Regenerative farming describes farming and grazing practices that, among other benefits, reverse climate change by rebuilding soil organic matter and restoring degraded soil biodiversity – resulting in both carbon drawdown and improving the water cycle.

This method of farming in general has been around for ages, but in the past several decades has often been pushed aside. This, along with proper care and diet for the animals, can work hand in hand to help improve our surrounding environment.

 # BEEF

DOES GRASS FED BEEF TASTE DIFFERENT THAN GRAIN FED BEEF?

Grass fed and finished beef is traditionally lower in fat than corn fed beef, since the cows are healthier! This can sometimes result in a milder flavor, but at Wild Pastures we counteract this by dry aging our beef. This allows for better flavor and easier cooking methods.

DOES GRASS FED BEEF NEED TO BE COOKED DIFFERENTLY?

Grass fed, dry aged beef tends to cook a bit faster than grain fed beef. We recommend keeping a close eye when cooking grass fed beef and using a meat thermometer to guarantee you don't cook it past your preference.

DOES GRASS FED BEEF LOOK DIFFERENT?

Sometimes grass fed beef can look slightly darker red in color than the meat you're used to. This is actually normal! This occurs when steaks are cut from primals (the cuts of meat that are separated right away from the animal). You will find that once it is thawed out, it will return to a beautiful reddish color.

TO WHAT INTERNAL TEMPERATURE SHOULD I COOK MY BEEF?

Rare- 120°F

Medium-rare - 130°F

Medium - 140°F

Medium-well - 150°F

Well-done - 160°F

WHAT IS THE BEST INTERNAL TEMPERATURE FOR GRASS FED BEEF?

While everyone has a different preference, the most popular temperature to cook grass fed beef is medium-rare. At about 130° - 140°F, the marbled fat begins to melt, adding a delicious flavor and tenderness. The exception is for tougher cuts like brisket or chuck roast, which should be cooked at a higher temperature until the meat begins to fall apart.

DO I NEED TO REST GRASS FED BEEF?

It's always important to let your grass fed beef rest directly after you remove it from cooking. This helps redistribute the juices throughout the meat, so it's perfectly moist and juicy every time.

Keep in mind that with thicker cuts, like ribeyes or strip steaks, the temperature can rise up to 5 degrees over a 10 minute rest period.

Roasts like prime rib can rise 10 degrees over a 30-40 minute rest. For this reason, we recommend taking these thicker cuts off of heat 5-10 degrees before your ideal temperature to avoid overcooking while resting.

 # CHICKEN

DOES PASTURE-RAISED CHICKEN TASTE DIFFERENT?

Pasture-raised chickens aren't "engineered" to be plump and juicy. These are natural chickens raised the way they were supposed to be, without harmful additives to fatten them up. As a result, you may notice tough or dry meat after cooking, but this can be easily solved by tenderizing.

HOW DO YOU TENDERIZE A WHOLE CHICKEN?

Before cooking place the chicken in a dish to catch any liquids. Cover loosely with plastic wrap and let it sit in your refrigerator for 2-5 days so the muscles can relax and the meat will become tender.

If you're cooking a frozen chicken, give it at least 2-3 days to thaw in the fridge for a similar result. A trick to know when a frozen chicken is fully thawed is the leg joints will easily wiggle as opposed to feeling stiff.

TO WHAT INTERNAL TEMPERATURE DO I NEED TO COOK THE CHICKEN?

165°F. For a whole chicken, cook until the thigh reaches a temperature of 170°F to guarantee the rest of the meat is at a safe temperature.

HOW CAN I MAKE MY CHICKEN MORE FLAVORFUL AND TENDER?

Since pasture-raised chickens haven't been injected with any kind of water, broth, salt, or chemical additives, they may seem less flavorful or tougher than the conventionally raised chicken. There's an easy solution! Brining or marinating.

FAQ

HOW DO I BRINE A CHICKEN?

Brining your chicken will give it a delicious, tender flavor without the harmful chemicals and additives conventional farms use. Simply soak your chicken in the brine in the fridge for at least 4 hours (or 8 hours for a whole bird). There are two types of brine: water and milk.

WATER BRINE - Saltwater brines are great for a whole chicken or chicken pieces. The base is salt, water and sugar, followed by water, herbs and spices you want to use.

MILK BRINE - Buttermilk brines are a Southern staple. If you are on a dairy-free diet, don't worry! You can use your favorite dairy-free milk combined with vinegar, or lemon to give it the acidity needed to tenderize the meat.

SHOULD I MARINATE MY CHICKEN?

If you're not brining, we always recommend marinating your chicken overnight before preparing. Use something slightly acidic, like lemon, lime, vinegar, wine, etc. to help loosen up the pasture-raised chickens' strong muscles from all those days of exercise.

 # PORK

IS PASTURE-RAISED PORK A LOT DIFFERENT FROM CONVENTIONALLY RAISED PORK?

Pasture-raised pork is often slightly leaner and much higher quality than conventional pork.

HOW SHOULD I COOK PASTURE-RAISED PORK?

Allow pasture-raised pork to come to room temperature before cooking. Allow it to rest for 5-10 minutes after cooking to keep the sweet, tender flavor.

WHAT INTERNAL TEMPERATURE SHOULD PORK REACH WHILE COOKING?

145°F.

SHOULD I MARINATE THE PORK?

We recommend marinating pork tenderloin overnight and cooking very quickly after marinating. Because this is such a tender, lean cut, watch it closely to avoid drying out.

HOW SHOULD I COOK A PASTURE-RAISED PORK ROAST?

Make sure you give pork roasts extra time to cook. We recommend roasting it for at least 6 hours in a slow cooker on low, or 2-3 hours in the oven at 325°F.

SHOULD I SEASON MY PASTURE-RAISED PORK?

Because this meat is leaner than the usual, conventionally raised meat, we recommend adding all your favorite seasonings. Pork is naturally flavorful and slightly sweet. We recommend keeping the seasoning simple. Use sea salt, thyme, rosemary, and your other favorite herbs for a delicious meal!

SEAFOOD

WHY DOES MY WILD-CAUGHT SALMON LOOK DIFFERENT?

Most people don't realize farm-raised salmon is naturally a gray-ish color, and the pink color is artificially added. With wild-caught salmon, the fish's color comes from its natural diet of krill and shrimp giving it its natural, pinkish hue.

TO WHAT TEMPERATURE SHOULD I COOK MY SEAFOOD?

Shrimp - 145°F

Salmon - 145°F

Cod - 145°F

Scallops - 125-130°F

SHOULD I MARINATE MY SEAFOOD?

Marinating seafood is a great way to add flavor. However, fish is often much more delicate than meat and should not marinade nearly as long. Aim for 30 minutes to an hour in the refrigerator if you opt to use a marinade when cooking seafood.

DO I NEED TO COOK WILD-CAUGHT FISH DIFFERENTLY THAN CONVENTIONALLY RAISED FISH?

In general, no. Wild-caught fish should cook very similarly to any fish you've cooked in the past. The slight difference is wild-caught salmon can be more delicate and cooks slightly faster. For this reason it should be watched closely, as it can easily become dry if overcooked.

PASTURE-RAISED CHICKEN

WHY FREE-RANGE ISN'T ENOUGH

Pasture-raised is NOT the same as free-range. Our chickens spend their lives on pastures eating their natural diet of bugs and forage. "Free-range" is not ideal as the birds are often kept indoors and never set foot on pasture. Pasture-raised chicken is more nutrient-dense and richer in flavor.

While other chickens are forced to remain indoors, our chickens are allowed to thrive and flourish outdoors in small flocks. "Organic chicken" can also be deceiving since there is no requirement for the birds to ever set foot on a pasture.

Wild Pastures' chickens freely roam open pastures. They are raised in the USA by small family farmers without antibiotics, steroids or hormones.

CREAMY CAULIFLOWER SOUP WITH BONE BROTH

PREP
15
MINUTES

COOK
40
MINUTES

TOTAL
55
MINUTES

SERVES
4

This low-carb creamy soup is full of the flavor you'd expect from potato soup, but with less carbs and a dose of vitamin C thanks to cauliflower. To add rich flavor with buttery notes, cauliflower, sweet onion and garlic are roasted in ghee until lightly browned, sealing in sweetness and toasty notes. To finish this soup off, smoky bacon and green onion are added for a bowl of comfort that is guilt-free!

INGREDIENTS:

- 3 cups chicken bone broth
- 1 large head of cauliflower, broken into florets
- 4 strips pasture-raised bacon
- 1 Tbsp. melted ghee
- 1 small sweet white onion, chopped
- 4 cloves garlic
- Pinch of nutmeg
- 1/2 tsp. sea salt
- 1/4 tsp. cracked pepper
- 1/4 cup chopped green onions or chives

EQUIPMENT:

- Immersion blender
- Baking sheet

DIRECTIONS:

1 Preheat oven to 375°F. Lay bacon on a parchment lined sheet tray. Bake until crispy, approximately 15 minutes. Chop bacon once cooled.

2 Increase oven temperature to 400°F. Place cauliflower and onion on a baking sheet. Drizzle with melted ghee and add garlic to the baking sheet. Toss to coat. Roast until vegetables have browned bits around edges, about 20-25 minutes.

3 Meanwhile, heat bone broth in a large stockpot over medium heat. Once boiling, add roasted cauliflower, onion, garlic, nutmeg, sea salt and black pepper. Turn heat off and purée using an immersion blender until cauliflower is mixed and broth is thick and creamy.

4 Ladle soup into bowls and top with bacon and chives.

BONE BROTH WITH A BOOST

PREP
5
MINUTES

COOK
3
HOURS

TOTAL
3
HOURS

SERVES
4

P · CERTIFIED PALEO K · KETO FRIENDLY · GLUTEN FREE · · DAIRY FREE ·

Bone broth is known for having a wide variety of health benefits. Weight loss, collagen for healthy skin, hair, and nails, gut health, and more. So we decided to take it and make it even better. With these additional ingredients, not only is it delicious, but it has added health benefits like a strong immune system, healthy inflammation levels, liver support, and more! Substitute butter with coconut oil or avocado oil to make it Paleo-friendly.

INGREDIENTS:

- 1 chicken back
- 4-5 cloves garlic (boosts the immune system)
- 1 tsp. grass fed butter, coconut or avocado oil
- 4 stalks celery, sliced in quarters (lowers inflammation, supports the liver)
- 2 whole carrots, sliced in quarters (beta carotene and antioxidants)
- 1/2 red or white onion sliced (reduce inflammation and heal infections, vitamin c helps boost immune system)
- Knuckle of ginger and/or turmeric (healthy inflammation)
- 4 cups water or organic chicken stock
- Salt and pepper to taste

EQUIPMENT:

- Large stovetop pot

DIRECTIONS:

1 Melt butter or cooking oil in a large pot on low-medium heat. Once melted, add garlic and onions. Cook until softened.

2 Add celery, carrots and ginger/turmeric and salt and pepper to taste. Sauté on medium until slightly cooked.

3 Add chicken back and water or stock then cover with a lid. Bring stock to a boil, then let simmer for 2-3 hours.

4 Let cool, then pour into a storage container (we recommend mason jars) using a sieve or some sort of filter to separate the bones from the broth. Store in the refrigerator.

5 Pour into a mug and lightly heat on stove when ready to drink.

CHICKEN PICCATA

PREP
10
MINUTES

COOK
24
MINUTES

TOTAL
34
MINUTES

SERVES
4

Thanks to the convenience of grain-free flours, enjoying the flavor of your favorite dishes doesn't mean sacrificing texture! Chicken Piccata is known for its light coating of flour that pairs perfectly with a buttery sauce. Instead of all-purpose flour, arrowroot flour stands in to dredge the chicken with its airy texture. Garlic, lemon and capers add mouthwatering aroma.

This evergreen recipe is hearty enough for a winter comfort food meal and yet also light and bright enough to serve during warmer months. To round out the dish, serve chicken over cauliflower mashed potatoes, sautéed mushroom or buttery spinach.

INGREDIENTS:

- 4 chicken breasts boneless/skinless
- 1/2 cup arrowroot flour
- 3 Tbsp. olive oil
- 3 Tbsp. butter
- 2 lemon
- 1/2 cup chicken stock
- 2 garlic cloves, minced
- 2 Tbsp. capers

- 1/4 cup parsley, chopped
- 1/2 tsp. sea salt
- 1/4 tsp. black pepper

EQUIPMENT:

- Large shallow bowl
- Large pan
- Wooden spatula

DIRECTIONS:

1 Reserve juice from 1 lemon and thinly slice the other. Set aside. Blot excess moisture off chicken using paper towel and slice chicken breasts in half lengthwise. In a shallow bowl, stir together arrowroot flour, sea salt and black pepper. Dredge chicken breasts in flour on both sides.

2 Heat 2 tablespoons of olive oil and 2 tablespoons of butter in a large pan over medium-high heat. Allow 2 minutes for pan to get very hot. Place 3-4 chicken breasts in pan. Brown for 4 minutes on each side. Transfer to a plate and cover to keep warm. Repeat with remaining chicken breasts. Transfer to plate.

3 Reduce heat to medium, add garlic and remaining butter and olive oil to pan. Add chicken stock, lemon juice and capers to pan. Scrape up any brown bits using a wooden spatula. Heat for 3 minutes. Add chicken breasts and lemon slices to pan and heat for 3 minutes longer. Serve hot garnished with fresh parsley.

CHICKEN VERDE SOUP

PREP
10
MINUTES

COOK
30
MINUTES

TOTAL
40
MINUTES

SERVES
6-8

Shredded chicken provides the backbone for this hearty soup that will leave you satisfied without feeling stuffed! That's because it is made with lean chicken and ample antioxidant rich vegetables in a slurp-worthy broth. Tomatillos add a tangy flavor to the soup while raw vegetables like avocado and sliced radishes finish it off for a recipe that is equally delicious in the summer or fall.

INGREDIENTS:

- 2 lbs. shredded chicken breasts
- 1 Tbsp. butter
- 2 tsp. minced garlic
- 1/2 cup chopped white onion
- 2 poblano peppers, minced
- 1 lb. tomatillos, peeled and chopped (3 cups chopped)
- 6 cups chicken stock
- 2 Tbsp. ground cumin
- 2 tsp. dried oregano
- 1/2 tsp. ground coriander
- 1 tsp. sea salt
- 1/2 cup chopped cilantro

   Optional toppings: sliced avocado, sliced radish, chopped cilantro, lime wedges

EQUIPMENT:

- Dutch oven

DIRECTIONS:

1 Heat butter over medium-high heat in a dutch oven and add peppers and onion. Sauté for 5 minutes. Stir in tomatillos and garlic. Continue to sauté for 5 minutes.

2 Add chicken stock, shredded chicken, cumin, coriander, oregano and sea salt. Bring to a boil and reduce heat to medium-low. Simmer for 20 minutes. Turn heat off and stir in cilantro. Ladle into bowls and garnish with desired toppings.

CREAMY CHICKEN VEGETABLE SOUP

PREP
10
MINUTES

COOK
27
MINUTES

TOTAL
37
MINUTES

SERVES
8

P CERTIFIED PALEO · CERTIFIED PALEO

K KETO FRIENDLY · KETO FRIENDLY

GLUTEN FREE · GLUTEN FREE · GLUTEN FREE

Nothing soothes on a chilly winter day quite like a hot bowl of soup. This delicious chicken soup is filling, yet light with antioxidants to boot! Best of all, it makes a large batch, perfect for reheating on busy days. This soup is very versatile, so feel free to use your preferred method of cooking the chicken; from grilled to slow-cooked. Shredded roasted whole chicken can also be used for cooked all day flavor.

TIP! *Be sure not to overheat soup as this can cause the arrowroot powder to separate from the broth, becoming thin again.*

INGREDIENTS:

- 1 lb. chicken breast, cooked/shredded
- 4 celery stalks, thinly sliced
- 2 medium carrots, thinly sliced
- 1 small sweet white onion, chopped
- 1 garlic clove, minced
- 2 cups baby portobello mushrooms, sliced
- 1 cup fresh spinach leaves
- 3 cups chicken stock
- 3 cups unsweetened almond milk
- 1/4 cup arrowroot powder

- 3 Tbsp. ghee
- 1 tsp. dried marjoram
- 2 sprigs fresh thyme
- 1 tsp. sea salt
- 1/4 tsp. black pepper

EQUIPMENT:

- 5 quart Dutch oven or stock pot
- Medium saucepan
- Spatula
- Whisk

DIRECTIONS:

1 Melt 1 tablespoon of ghee in a large stock pot or dutch oven over medium heat. Add celery, carrot and onion. Cover and cook 5 minutes. Add garlic and mushrooms to pot. Stir well, cover and cook an additional 5 minutes. Add chicken stock and thyme sprigs to pot and bring to a boil. Reduce heat to low.

2 In a separate medium saucepan, heat remaining 2 tablespoons of ghee over low heat until melted. Gradually whisk in half of the arrowroot powder to make a roux. Break up any clumps. Gradually add almond milk, whisking constantly until fully incorporated. Whisk in remaining arrowroot powder. Continue to heat until boiling, whisking occasionally until almond milk is thickened and creamy, about 5 minutes.

3 Pour almond milk mixture into the pot with vegetables and stir well. Add chicken and marjoram. Bring to a low boil and reduce heat to simmer for 10 minutes. Remove thyme and discard. Add spinach and allow to wilt for 2 minutes. Season with salt and pepper. Serve hot.

FAJITA VEGETABLE BAKE

PREP
5
MINUTES

COOK
40
MINUTES

TOTAL
45
MINUTES

SERVES
4

Want all the deliciousness of fajitas without dealing with a scorching hot cast iron pan and splattering oil?

This Fajita Vegetable Bake is exactly what you need. It's great for entertaining since it doesn't need a lot of supervision while it cooks. You can serve it with cauliflower rice, grain rice, or tortillas, to suit everyone's dietary preferences.

INGREDIENTS:

- 3 - 4 (1 1/2 lbs.) chicken breasts, cut into thick strips
- 2 bell peppers, cut into strips
- 1 red onion, thinly sliced
- 1 Tbsp. chili powder
- 1 tsp. ground cumin
- 1 tsp. paprika
- 1/4 tsp. cayenne pepper
- 1/4 tsp. garlic powder
- 3 Tbsp. coconut oil
- 1 tsp. sea salt
- 1 tsp. fresh cracked pepper

EQUIPMENT:

- Casserole dish
- Parchment paper

DIRECTIONS:

1 Preheat oven to 375°F. Make the fajita seasoning by whisking together the chili powder, cumin, paprika, cayenne, garlic powder, salt and pepper.

2 In a deep casserole dish, drizzle with 1 tablespoon of coconut oil and lay out the chicken pieces. Coat with about half of the fajita seasoning. Layer the pepper and onion mixture on top, then drizzle with the remaining coconut oil and fajita seasoning.

3 Cover with parchment paper and bake for 30-40 minutes until the chicken is cooked and the juices run clear. Serve over your choice of cauliflower rice or leafy greens.

OVEN 'FRIED' CHICKEN BREAST

PREP
10
MINUTES

COOK
50
MINUTES

TOTAL
60
MINUTES

SERVES
2

P CERTIFIED PALEO

K KETO FRIENDLY

GLUTEN FREE

DAIRY FREE

If you're longing for the texture of fried chicken, but don't want to sacrifice health, nuts are the answer! They take the place of breadcrumbs or traditional flour for a Paleo-friendly 'fried' chicken. We used pecans for this recipe, but almonds or even cashews would work. Serve chicken hot alongside coleslaw, cucumber salad or mashed cauliflower.

TIP! *Be sure not to overblend the nut mixture, or the oils will start to draw from pecans resulting in a sticky mixture.*

INGREDIENTS:

- 2 - 8 oz bone-in chicken breasts
- 1 egg
- 2 Tbsp. arrowroot flour
- 1 cup raw, unsalted pecan halves
- 1/2 tsp. dried dill
- 1/4 tsp. dried thyme
- 1/4 tsp. onion powder
- 1/2 tsp. sea salt
- 1/8 tsp. black pepper

EQUIPMENT:

- Baking sheet
- Parchment paper
- Food processor
- 3 shallow bowls

DIRECTIONS:

1 Preheat oven to 350°F and line a baking sheet with parchment paper. Combine pecans, dill, thyme, onion powder, sea salt and black pepper in a food processor. Pulse until finely crumbled. Transfer mixture to a large shallow bowl.

2 In two separate shallow bowls, whisk egg in one and add arrowroot powder to the other. Set up a station with the arrowroot powder bowl first, followed by the egg bowl and finally the pecan mixture. Dredge the top of each chicken breast in arrowroot flour followed by egg, shaking off any excess egg. Place chicken breast skin side down in the pecan mixture and press to adhere pecans. Turn chicken breast and use hands to firmly press pecan mixture onto any areas that aren't coated. Transfer to prepared baking sheet and repeat with remaining chicken breast. Bake chicken for 45-50 minutes or until top is golden brown and juices run clear.

THAI STIR FRY

PREP
5-8
MINUTES

COOK
12-15
MINUTES

TOTAL
23
MINUTES

SERVES
4

P K (Certified Paleo · Keto Friendly · Gluten Free · Dairy Free)

Stir fry is one of the quickest, yet healthiest, dinners to whip up in a jiffy. This recipe features traditional stir fry veggies, along with antioxidant-rich coconut oil, a sweet and salty Thai sauce that subs creamy cashew butter for peanut butter (perfect if you're peanut-free!), and tangy lime alongside succulent chicken.

INGREDIENTS:

- 2 chicken breasts, cut into bite-size pieces
- 2 large carrots, cut into matchsticks
- 1 purple cabbage, shredded
- 1 Tbsp. avocado oil
- 1 Tbsp. coconut aminos
- 2 shallots, thinly sliced
- 5 garlic cloves, minced
- 2 Tbsp. fresh ginger, minced
- 4 lime wedges
- Scallions and cilantro for garnish

For Thai Sauce:

- 3 Tbsp. rice vinegar
- 2 tbsp sesame oil
- 3 Tbsp. coconut aminos
- 1/2 cup cashew butter
- 1 Tbsp. raw honey
- 1 Tbsp. ginger paste

EQUIPMENT:

- Large sauté pan

DIRECTIONS:

1 Cube the chicken into bite-size pieces and toss with 1 Tbsp. of coconut aminos. In a large skillet, heat avocado oil over medium-high heat and sauté the chicken until browned and cooked through, about 6 minutes. Remove chicken and set aside.

2 Add to the skillet the shallots, carrots, ginger, garlic, and cabbage and quickly sauté over high heat until the veggies are par cooked, but still a bit crunchy. Stir frequently.

3 To make the sauce, whisk together all of the sauce ingredients until smooth. Add the chicken back to the skillet with the veggies and pour the sauce over the mixture and heat through.

4 Serve with scallions, cilantro and a lime wedge.

WALDORF CHICKEN SALAD

PREP
10
MINUTES

COOK
35
MINUTES

TOTAL
60
MINUTES

SERVES
4-6

P — CERTIFIED PALEO

K — KETO FRIENDLY

GLUTEN FREE

DAIRY FREE

If you're someone who's always looking for a great meal prep recipe, this one's for you. It lasts for a few days in the refrigerator and actually gets better with time as all the flavors blend beautifully together.

Make this on a warm spring or summer day to enjoy with crackers on a picnic, in butter lettuce wraps, or simply on its own.

INGREDIENTS:

- 2 chicken breasts

- 1 Tbsp. avocado oil

- 1/4 red cabbage, thinly shredded

- 6 celery stalks, 1/2" dice

- 2 crisp, tart apples (like granny smith or pink lady), cored and thinly sliced

- 1/2 red onion, thinly sliced

- 2 Tbsp. fresh dill, finely chopped

- 1/4 cup hazelnuts (can sub walnuts), toasted and chopped

- 1/4 cup golden raisins

- 1 cup paleo aioli or mayonnaise (like Primal Kitchen Avocado Mayo)

- 2 Tbsp. lemon juice

- Sea salt and fresh cracked pepper

- Fresh chives, for garnish

EQUIPMENT:

- Baking sheet

- Large mixing bowl

- Parchment paper

DIRECTIONS:

1 Preheat oven to 350°F. Rinse and pat dry the chicken breasts. Drizzle with avocado oil and season both sides with salt and pepper.

2 Bake on a parchment-lined sheet pan for 30-35 minutes, or until cooked through and juices run clear. Remove from the oven and allow to cool completely.

3 While the chicken is in the oven, prepare the vegetables and herbs.

4 After the chicken has completely cooled, shred the meat with your hands and add to a large mixing bowl. Combine the cabbage, celery, apples, red onion, chicken, aioli, dill, raisins, and lemon juice. Season with salt and pepper to taste (about 1 teaspoon of each).

5 Garnish with toasted hazelnuts or walnuts and fresh chives. Serve right away, or store in the refrigerator for later. This keeps well for a few days and makes for a great snack or lunch on the go!

YELLOW CHICKEN CURRY

PREP
10
MINUTES

COOK
28
MINUTES

TOTAL
38
MINUTES

SERVES
6

Put away the takeout menu! This Paleo spin on classic curry combines all the goodness of takeout with the health benefits of pasture-raised chicken in a medley of vitamin-rich vegetables and creamy coconut broth. To add even more vegetables to the mix, this curry is best served over riced cauliflower or zucchini noodles. This recipe makes a large batch, perfect for reheating during the week or feeding a crowd.

INGREDIENTS:

- 1 lb. boneless skinless chicken breast, cubed
- 1 tsp. virgin coconut oil
- 1 red bell pepper, chopped
- 1/2 cup sweet white onion, chopped
- 1 baby eggplant, chopped
- 3 Tbsp. yellow curry paste
- 1 (14 oz.) can coconut cream
- 1 cup chicken stock
- 2 cups broccoli florets
- 1 handful fresh basil leaves, torn
- 1 lime, cut into wedges
- 6 cups cauliflower rice or zucchini noodles for serving

EQUIPMENT:

- Large sauté pan

DIRECTIONS:

1 Melt coconut oil in a large sauté pan over medium heat for 2 minutes. Add chicken and lightly brown for 5 minutes, stirring occasionally. Add bell pepper and onion, continue to cook for 3 minutes longer.

2 Add eggplant and curry paste to the pan. Stir well to coat chicken and vegetables. Stir in coconut cream and chicken stock. Bring to a boil and reduce heat to simmer. Simmer for 15 minutes. Add broccoli and basil. Simmer 3 minutes longer.

3 Serve over cauliflower rice or zucchini noodles with lime wedges.

BALSAMIC ROASTED CHICKEN LEGS WITH SUN-DRIED TOMATOES

PREP
10
MINUTES

COOK
45
MINUTES

TOTAL
55
MINUTES

SERVES
4

This Italian inspired dish will transport you to the rolling hills of Tuscany in no time at all. With only 10 minutes of prep work, this meal practically makes itself. In the end you're left with juicy chicken legs in a delicious Balsamic and sun-dried tomato sauce that you'll want to pour over the whole meal. Delicious served with cauliflower rice, a green vegetable side, or simply on its own!

INGREDIENTS:

- 4 chicken legs (drumsticks)
- 2 green onions, sliced thin
- 2 Tbsp. Balsamic vinegar
- 1 tsp. dried oregano
- 1 garlic clove, minced
- 1/4 cup yellow onion, diced thin
- 1/4 cup olive oil
- 1/4 cup sun-dried tomatoes, chopped
- Sea salt and pepper, to taste

EQUIPMENT:

- Large baking dish or pan

DIRECTIONS:

1 Preheat oven to 350°F.

2 In a large bowl, combine sun-dried tomatoes, Balsamic vinegar, oregano, onion, garlic, and olive oil.

3 In a baking dish, arrange the drumsticks in a single layer and pour the tomato mixture on top. Season with salt and pepper to taste.

4 Sprinkle half of the green onions over the chicken, and bake for 45 minutes, or until the chicken is cooked through.

5 Remove and sprinkle the rest of the green onions over the drumsticks before serving.

GREEK BRAISED CHICKEN LEGS

PREP
10
MINUTES

COOK
48
MINUTES

TOTAL
58
MINUTES

SERVES
2

Chicken legs are the ideal cut of chicken to braise, because they're full of juicy dark meat and the skin browns beautifully sealing in the aromatic herbs. They're an eat-with-your-hands, no-frills cut that turns this otherwise fancy recipe into a great game day or party appetizer. Serve hot alongside cauliflower rice or traditional rice for a complete meal.

TIP! *Chicken thighs can be substituted for chicken legs if desired.*

INGREDIENTS:

- 2 lbs. chicken legs or thighs
- 1 Tbsp. butter
- 1 lemon, sliced
- 1 tsp. fresh thyme leaves
- 1/2 tsp. dried oregano
- 3 cloves garlic, halved
- 2 shallots, halved
- 1/2 cup pitted greek olives

- 1 cup chicken stock
- 1/2 tsp. sea salt
- 1/4 tsp. black pepper

EQUIPMENT:

- Medium sauté pan or cast iron skillet
- Wooden spatula

DIRECTIONS:

1 Preheat oven to 350°F. Remove chicken legs from package and pat dry with paper towel. Season with sea salt and black pepper. Melt butter over medium heat in a medium sauté pan for 2 minutes. Add chicken legs to pan and lightly brown for 3 minutes, turn and brown an additional 3 minutes.

2 Set chicken legs aside on a plate. Pour chicken stock into pan and scrape up any browned bits from pan with a wooden spatula. Return chicken legs to pan and season with thyme and oregano. Add lemon slices, garlic, shallots, Greek olives to pan. Transfer to oven and braise for 30-35 minutes. If desired, turn oven to broil at the end for 5 minutes or until skin is crisp. Serve hot.

CRISPY TAJIN CHICKEN SKINS

PREP
10
MINUTES

COOK
30
MINUTES

TOTAL
40
MINUTES

SERVES
2

P CERTIFIED PALEO · CERTIFIED PALEO

K KETO FRIENDLY · KETO FRIENDLY

GLUTEN FREE · GLUTEN FREE

DAIRY FREE · DAIRY FREE

For a Paleo-friendly alternative to chips and popcorn, these crispy oven-fried chicken skins will curb a craving. They are also Keto compliant and super easy to prepare using Tajin seasoning. This Mexican spice is a mix of salt, chili powder, and dehydrated lime, giving the perfect flavor for movie time munching. Dip these crispy cracklins in guacamole, salsa, or Paleo-friendly ranch!

INGREDIENTS:

- 8 raw pieces of chicken skin from thigh or breast meat
- 1 1/2 tsp. Tajin seasoning

EQUIPMENT:

- Baking sheet

DIRECTIONS:

1 Preheat oven to 375ºF. Use paper towels to dry chicken skins, blotting any moisture from the skin.

2 Stretch chicken skins on a parchment paper lined baking sheet with 1-inch of space between them. Sprinkle with 1 teaspoon of Tajin seasoning. Bake for 25-30 minutes or until chicken skins are golden brown and crispy. Cool at room temperature for 5 minutes.

3 Serve warm sprinkled with remaining Tajin seasoning if desired.

CATANZARO HERBED CHICKEN SKILLET

PREP
15
MINUTES

COOK
20
MINUTES

TOTAL
35
MINUTES

SERVES
3-4

P CERTIFIED PALEO · CERTIFIED PALEO

K KETO FRIENDLY · KETO FRIENDLY

GLUTEN FREE · GLUTEN FREE · GLUTEN FREE

DAIRY FREE · DAIRY FREE · DAIRY FREE

This one pan meal makes cleanup a breeze! Chicken thighs are one of the easiest cuts of chicken to cook, because they are hard to overcook and remain deliciously juicy. Paired with a combination of herbs and spices, this dish will have you wanting seconds.

INGREDIENTS:

- 6-8 chicken thighs
- 1 lemon, zested and juiced
- 3 Tbsp. avocado oil, divided
- 1/2 Tbsp. basil
- 1/2 tsp. thyme
- 1/4 tsp. marjoram
- 1/4 tsp. rosemary
- 1/4 tsp. oregano
- 2 garlic cloves, minced
- 1 yellow onion, chopped
- 1 zucchini, sliced thick in half circles

- 1 small eggplant, cubed
- 1 red bell pepper, chopped
- 1 large heirloom or similar tomato, seeds removed and chopped
- 3/4 tsp. salt, divided
- 3/4 tsp. cracked pepper, divided
- Fresh rosemary, for garnish

EQUIPMENT:

- Large skillet

DIRECTIONS:

1 Season chicken thighs with lemon juice and zest, and 1/2 teaspoon salt and pepper. Let marinate at least 10-15 minutes.

2 Meanwhile, toss veggies with remaining salt and pepper, 2 teaspoons avocado oil, basil, thyme, marjoram, rosemary, oregano and garlic. Set aside.

3 Heat skillet over medium high heat. Add avocado oil. Brown chicken thighs on both sides, approximately 5-7 minutes per side. Remove from pan.

4 Add veggies to the skillet chicken was cooked in. Cook over medium heat, stirring occasionally, until soft.

5 Return chicken to the skillet. Top with rosemary garnish.

MOROCCAN CHICKEN STEW

PREP
10
MINUTES

COOK
68
MINUTES

TOTAL
78
MINUTES

SERVES
4

Moroccan cooking is full of unexpected flavors. With the addition of dried fruits, nuts and warm spices, these dishes are never boring. This chicken thigh stew satisfies a sweet-savory craving and is full of cauliflower and carrots for a one-pan meal that feeds a crowd. Substitute butter with coconut oil or avocado oil to make it Paleo-friendly.

INGREDIENTS:

- 4 large bone-in pasture-raised chicken thighs

- 4 cups chicken bone broth

- 2 Tbsp. unsalted butter or ghee

- 3 cups cauliflower florets

- 2 cups peeled chopped carrots

- 1/2 cup chopped sweet white onion

- 3 garlic cloves, minced

- 2 Tbsp. tomato paste

- 1/3 cup chopped, dried, unsweetened apricots

- 1 tsp. dried marjoram

- 1 tsp. ground turmeric

- 1 tsp. cumin

- 1/4 tsp. cinnamon

- 1 tsp. sea salt

- 1/4 tsp. cracked black pepper

- 1/2 cup chopped cilantro

- 1/3 cup chopped raw pistachios

EQUIPMENT:

- Large heavy pan

DIRECTIONS:

1 Heat butter over medium-high heat in a large heavy pan. Once butter is sizzling, add chicken thighs skin side down and brown for 6 minutes.

2 Set chicken aside on a plate and reduce heat to medium. Add apricots, garlic, onion, carrots and cauliflower. Cook for 2 minutes. Stir in marjoram, cumin, turmeric, cinnamon, tomato paste and bone broth. Bring to a boil. Add chicken thighs back to the pan and season with salt and pepper.

3 Cover with the lid cracked slightly and reduce heat to medium low. Cook for 1 hour. Transfer chicken thighs to serving bowls and ladle vegetables and broth on top. Garnish with cilantro and chopped pistachios.

CHICKEN CURRY SOUP

PREP
5
MINUTES

COOK
15
MINUTES

TOTAL
20
MINUTES

SERVES
4

CERTIFIED PALEO · **P** · CERTIFIED PALEO   KETO FRIENDLY · **K** · KETO FRIENDLY   GLUTEN FREE · GLUTEN FREE   DAIRY FREE · DAIRY FREE

Curry and noodles without a lot of carbs? Welcome to Heaven. This curry soup uses low-carb and gluten-free Shirataki noodles for richness and texture. Perfectly seared chicken and spices round out mouthfuls of flavor. If you're craving noodles but don't want to load up on carbs, this recipe is for you!

INGREDIENTS:

- 1 lb. chicken thighs (boneless/skinless), cut into thin strips
- 1 Tbsp. avocado oil
- 5 Tbsp. red curry paste
- 1 1/2 cups chicken broth
- 1/2 cup water
- 1 cup coconut milk
- 2 tsp. sea salt
- 1 package Shirataki noodles, rinsed well and drained
- 1/2 cup cilantro, chopped

EQUIPMENT:

- Large pot

DIRECTIONS:

1 Heat avocado oil in a large pot over medium-high heat and add the chicken. Cook until lightly browned and remove from pan.

2 In the same pot add the curry paste and stir for about a minute until it becomes fragrant. Add broth, water, coconut milk and salt and bring to a boil. Return the chicken to the pot and continue cooking at a simmer for about 10 minutes.

3 Divide the noodles between 4 bowls and ladle the soup into each bowl. Garnish with cilantro.

CHICKEN VEGGIE BOWL WITH CURRIED CASHEW CREAM

PREP
10
MINUTES

COOK
40
MINUTES

TOTAL
50
MINUTES

SERVES
3-4

When you're craving something creamy, but don't want to overdo it on dairy, this cashew cream chicken veggie bowl is the way to go! Made with juicy chicken thighs and a variety of vegetables, this dish feels indulgent but is loaded with nutrients.

INGREDIENTS:

- 6-8 chicken thighs
- 1-2 Tbsp. coconut oil (divided)
- 2 cups broccoli, broken down into florets
- 2 cups Brussels sprouts, ends trimmed and cut in quarters
- 2 cups cauliflower, broken down into florets
- 1/2 cup carrots, shredded
- 1/2 cup cashews, toasted
- 2 tsp. garlic powder (divided)
- 2 tsp. coriander
- 2 tsp. cumin
- Salt and cracked pepper to taste
- Cilantro, for garnish

For Curried Cashew Cream:

- 1 1/2 cups cashews, soaked at least 1 hour
- 1 Tbsp. lemon juice
- 1 garlic clove
- 1 tsp. coriander
- 2 tsp. curry powder
- Pinch cayenne pepper
- Water - as needed

EQUIPMENT:

- Baking tray
- Blender or food processor

DIRECTIONS:

1 Preheat oven to 350°F. Place chicken on an oven-proof sheet tray or baking dish. Coat with coconut oil, cracked pepper, and salt. Bake for 15-20 minutes or until chicken liquids run clear. Remove from oven and slice into strips.

2 Increase oven temperature to 375°F. In a medium bowl, toss broccoli with coconut oil. Sprinkle with salt, pepper, and 1/3 of the garlic powder, coriander, and cumin. Repeat this process with Brussels sprouts and cauliflower. Lay veggies (except carrots), out separately on lined sheet trays. Roasting separately will help veggies cook evenly. Roast 10-20 minutes, cooking Brussels sprouts the longest. Veggies should have browned bits around the corners, but not be mushy.

3 Drain and rinse cashews. Add to a blender, along with remaining curried cashew cream ingredients. Blend until smooth, adding water if necessary.

4 Serve chicken on top of roasted veggies, with curried cashew cream, shredded carrots, cilantro, and toasted cashews.

GREEN GODDESS CHICKEN VEGGIE BOWLS

PREP
5-10
MINUTES

COOK
48
MINUTES

TOTAL
40
MINUTES

SERVES
4

If you want a meal loaded with protein and healthy veggies, but not your same old chicken and veggies, look no further. Thanks to the flavorful avocado-tahini sauce, your usual chicken, rice, and veggies dish has been reborn!

INGREDIENTS:

- 4 - 6 chicken thighs or 2 large chicken breasts
- 1 1/2 cups Brussels sprouts
- 2 zucchinis
- 1 1/2 cups broccoli florets
- 4 cups riced cauliflower or cooked quinoa
- 3 1/2 Tbsp. avocado oil, divided
- Sea salt, pepper and garlic powder to taste

For Sauce:

- 1 avocado
- 2 scallions
- 1 cup basil

- 1/2 cup cilantro
- 1/2 cup parsley
- 1 garlic clove
- 1/4 cup tahini
- 2 Tbsp. lemon juice
- Splash of apple cider vinegar
- 2-4 Tbsp. of water

EQUIPMENT:

- Medium sauté pan or cast iron skillet
- Wooden spatula
- Parchment paper

DIRECTIONS:

1 Preheat oven to 375°F. Chop the Brussels sprouts, zucchini and broccoli into similarly sized pieces. Toss with 1 1/2 Tbsp. avocado oil, salt, pepper and garlic powder to taste.

2 Roast on a parchment lined baking sheet for about 20-30 minutes until browned and crispy.

3 Toss 1 Tbsp. of avocado oil with cauliflower (or quinoa), and bake on a parchment lined baking sheet for about 10 minutes.

4 Heat a large skillet with the remaining avocado oil, and season the chicken with salt, pepper and garlic powder. Brown the chicken on both sides. Cover and cook until opaque about 5-10 minutes depending on cut used turning occasionally.

5 While chicken is cooking, make the sauce by combining all ingredients in a food processor. Blend on high until it forms the texture of hummus/dressing. Add more water if a thinner consistency is desired.

6 Serve the veggies and chicken over the cauliflower rice or quinoa. Drizzle with sauce or serve it on the side.

SPINACH ARTICHOKE CHICKEN THIGHS

PREP
5
MINUTES

COOK
25
MINUTES

TOTAL
30
MINUTES

SERVES
4

Dinner is ready in under an hour with easy cleanup thanks to this one-pan recipe that serves four! The sauce is made in the pan after browning chicken for an ultra rich flavor that smothers the chicken thighs. Best of all, there's artichokes and chicken for a complete meal. Chicken breast or even pork chops would also work in this recipe. And, it can be served over cauliflower rice or traditional white rice to beef up the dish.

INGREDIENTS:

- 4 pasture-raised bone-in chicken thighs
- 2 Tbsp. grass fed butter (divided)
- 1 cup halved artichoke hearts (canned in water)
- 1 cup spinach
- 1 tsp. minced garlic
- 1 tsp. dried thyme
- 1/2 cup chicken stock
- 1 cup unsweetened almond milk
- 2 tsp. tapioca starch
- 1/2 tsp. sea salt
- 1/4 tsp. black pepper

EQUIPMENT:

- Large sauté pan
- Whisk

DIRECTIONS:

1 Heat 1 tablespoon of butter over medium heat in a large sauté pan.

2 Blot chicken thighs with paper towel to remove excess moisture and season with salt and pepper.

3 Brown chicken thighs on each side for 5 minutes. Set chicken thighs aside on a plate.

4 Reduce heat to medium-low. Add garlic and remaining butter to pan. Heat for 15 seconds to brown garlic. Stir in chicken stock and use a wooden spatula to scrape up any brown bits on pan.

5 Stir in almond milk and thyme. Bring to a simmer, then whisk in tapioca starch until slightly thickened.

6 Add artichokes, spinach and chicken thighs to pan. Simmer for 15 minutes or until chicken thighs are cooked through. Serve hot.

TANDOORI CHICKEN THIGH KEBABS

PREP
10
MINUTES

MARINATE
1-8
HOURS

COOK
20
MINUTES

TOTAL
90
MINUTES

SERVES
4

P CERTIFIED PALEO **K** KETO FRIENDLY GLUTEN FREE DAIRY FREE

Grilled chicken kebabs get smothered in a rich coconut marinade in this Indian inspired recipe. Coconut milk steps in for yogurt to keep these skewers Paleo and dairy-free while sealing in the aromatic spices. The high heat of grilling creates a light char that leaves behind a depth of flavor that is second to none.

Pasture-raised chicken thighs grill up tender and juicy locking in the flavor of both light and dark meat. Chicken breasts can also be used if preferred. *To keep this recipe Paleo, serve over steamed cauliflower rice or grain-free tabouli.*

INGREDIENTS:

- 3 lbs. boneless, skinless chicken thighs
- 1/2 cup canned unsweetened coconut milk
- 1 tsp. fresh ginger, minced
- 2 tsp. cumin
- 2 tsp. coconut sugar
- 1 tsp. paprika
- 1/2 tsp. turmeric
- 1/2 tsp. sea salt
- Avocodo oil or tallow
- 1/4 tsp. garlic powder
- 1/4 tsp. cinnamon
- 1/4 tsp. black pepper

EQUIPMENT:

- Medium mixing bowl
- 4 (8-10 inch) metal skewers
- Grill or grill pan

DIRECTIONS:

1 Slice chicken thighs into 3 inch pieces and place into a medium mixing bowl. Sprinkle spices and fresh ginger over chicken and pour coconut milk on top. Use hands to thoroughly mix, coating chicken thighs evenly. Cover and refrigerate for 1-8 hours.

2 Preheat grill or grill pan over medium-high heat and lightly grease with avocado oil or tallow. While grill heats, slide chicken thigh pieces onto 4 metal skewers.

3 Place kebabs on the grill and cook for 8-10 minutes. Turn and grill an additional 8-10 minutes. Serve hot.

CHIMICHURRI CHICKEN WINGS WITH RANCH

PREP
10
MINUTES

COOK
50
MINUTES

TOTAL
60
MINUTES

SERVES
4-6

Ranch is back! The drool-worthy way it combines with its new sauce friend, chimichurri, on juicy chicken wings is one for the books. And don't worry: no grill needed to get these babies crispy and flavorful.

INGREDIENTS:

- 2lbs chicken wings

  For Chimichurri Sauce:

- 1 bunch cilantro, thick stems removed
- 1/4 cup olive oil
- 1 tsp. lemon juice
- 1 Tbsp. red wine vinegar
- 1 tsp. sea salt
- Pepper, to taste
- 1 tsp. minced garlic

  For Dairy and Gluten-free Ranch Sauce:

- 3/4 cup avocado oil
- 1 whole egg, at room temperature
- 1/4 cup full fat canned coconut milk
- 2 Tbsp. chopped fresh dill

- 2 Tbsp. chopped fresh chives
- 2 Tbsp. chopped fresh cilantro
- 1 tsp. stone-ground mustard
- 1 Tbsp. red wine vinegar
- 1 tsp. lemon juice
- 3/4 tsp. garlic powder
- 3/4 tsp. onion powder
- 1/2 tsp. sea salt
- 1/4 tsp. pepper

EQUIPMENT:

- Immersion blender
- Food processor
- 1-2 baking sheets (optional: raised wire rack)
- Parchment paper (optional)

1. Begin with the chimichurri sauce by combining the cilantro, garlic, vinegar, lemon juice, salt, and pepper in a food processor, until completely chopped. Add in the olive oil until all the ingredients are well incorporated. Reserve 1/4 cup, setting aside for later.

2. Pat the chicken wings dry and place in a large bowl. Cover with chimichurri sauce and mix into the wings with your hands. (Optional: you can marinate this however long you like up to one day. If you do, place in a sealable bag in the fridge until you're ready to cook).

3. Preheat oven to 375°F. Bake on a baking sheet lined with parchment paper (if you don't have a raised wire sheet) in a single layer for 45-50 minutes, or until cooked through. To get crispy skins, broil on high for a few minutes before removing.

4. While wings are cooking, prepare the ranch sauce. Place all ranch ingredients minus the herbs in the bottom of a tall glass cup or wide-mouth mason jar, adding the egg and all the other ingredients first, followed by the oil last. Make sure the container can hold at least two cups!

5. Let the ingredients settle at the bottom of your jar, then place the immersion blender all the way to the bottom of the jar and blend. Move the blender around in the bottom of the cup, as well as up and down slightly; however, don't pull it out of the mixture. This can cause plenty of splatters! The sauce should be completely blended in about 30 seconds. When done, add in herbs on top of the mayo, then pulse until all the ingredients are completely mixed. Season with salt and pepper as desired.

6. When the wings are done, remove from the oven and let cool before serving with ranch.

CITRUS CACAO CHILI CHICKEN WINGS

PREP
5
MINUTES

MARINATE
12-24
HOURS

COOK
40
MINUTES

TOTAL
45
MINUTES

SERVES
3-4

Take your game day eats up a notch with Wild Pastures chicken wings! This flavorful wing recipe gets a little extra zest from the tangy orange juice, slightly sweet cacao, and spicy chipotle. It's like a flavor explosion everyone is sure to love! Serve these for the next big game or enjoy as a weekday dinner.

INGREDIENTS:

- 2 lbs chicken wings
- 1 cup organic orange juice
- 2 Tbsp. coconut flour
- 1/4 cup almond flour
- 2 tsp. salt, divided
- 2 tsp. cacao powder
- 1 tsp. chipotle powder
- 2 tsp. chili flakes
- Zest from 1 large orange (divided)

EQUIPMENT:

- Parchment-lined baking sheet with rack

DIRECTIONS:

1 Add orange juice and 1 teaspoon salt to a covered bowl or ziploc bag. Let marinate overnight or 24 hours.

2 Heat oven to 350°F. Combine thoroughly the coconut flour, almond flour, 1 teaspoon salt, cacao powder, chipotle powder, chili flakes and 1/2 of the orange zest in a bowl. Transfer to a bag or lidded container, add the wings into the powder, and shake well to coat.

3 Lay out on a rack over a baking sheet. Bake for 40 minutes, then remove and serve. Garnish with additional orange zest.

ROASTED JERK CHICKEN WITH ROASTED PURPLE SWEET POTATOES

PREP
5
MINUTES

COOK
30
MINUTES

TOTAL
35
MINUTES

SERVES
3-4

Slightly spicy, slightly sweet. These jerk chicken wings are the perfect way to spice up a weeknight dinner or serve at your next cookout. Purple sweet potatoes have a rich, slightly wine-like flavor that pairs nicely with the jerk chicken.

INGREDIENTS:

- 2 lbs chicken wings
- 2 Tbsp. baking powder
- 2 Tbsp. avocado or olive oil
- 1 Tbsp. garlic powder
- 1 1/2 tsp. onion powder
- 2 tsp. dried parsley
- 1 1/2 tsp. allspice
- 2 tsp. cayenne pepper
- 1/2 tsp. cinnamon

- 1 tsp. smoked paprika
- 1/2 tsp. chili pepper flakes
- 2-3 purple sweet potatoes, sliced into 1" thick disks
- 2 tsp. sea salt
- 1 tsp. black pepper
- Green onions and lime for garnish

EQUIPMENT:

- Baking sheets

DIRECTIONS:

1 Preheat oven to 425°F. Add 1 tablespoon avocado or olive oil to coat wings. Combine all the spices in a small bowl to make jerk seasoning. Rub seasoning on wings then place onto a parchment lined baking sheet.

2 Slice sweet potatoes, coat in 1 tablespoon avocado or olive oil, then place on another baking sheet.

3 Bake wings for 15 minutes, then flip and bake for another 15 minutes. Bake the sweet potato slices simultaneously, until tender with a fork.

4 Remove from oven, garnish with green onions, and serve with lime.

SWEET + SPICY PALEO CHICKEN WINGS WITH COCONUT DIP

PREP
10
MINUTES

COOK
40
MINUTES

TOTAL
50
MINUTES

SERVES
4

When it comes to enjoying chicken wings on a Paleo diet, there's always one big issue. The dip. Ranch and blue cheese are the traditional choices but are clearly not Paleo compliant. Enter: coconut dip. This creamy coconut sauce might just become a staple accompaniment when you make chicken wings - Paleo or not!

INGREDIENTS:

- 1 lb chicken wings
- 3 Tbsp. arrowroot starch
- 1/4 cup apple cider vinegar
- 1/4 cup honey
- 3/4 tsp. garlic powder
- 3/4 tsp. hot pepper flakes
- 2 tsp. tomato paste
- Salt to taste
- Celery for side dipping (optional)

For Coconut Dip:

- 1/2 cup homemade mayo (recipe included opposite) or purchased paleo mayo
- 3 Tbsp. coconut cream
- 1/2 tsp. garlic powder
- 1/2 tsp. onion powder
- 2 tsp. dried chives
- 1/4 tsp. dried dill
- 3/4 tsp. fresh lemon juice
- 1/8—1/4 tsp. salt

EQUIPMENT:

- Baking sheet
- Mixing bowl for sauces
- Parchment paper

DIRECTIONS:

1 Preheat oven to 425°F. Add arrowroot and chicken wings to a ziploc bag and shake so that chicken is fully coated. Place chicken directly onto a parchment-lined baking sheet. Bake for 30 minutes, flipping halfway through, until chicken is thoroughly cooked.

2 While the wings are baking, prepare the sauces. For the sweet and spicy sauce, mix the vinegar, honey, garlic powder, salt, and hot pepper flakes in a bowl until well blended.

3 Put the mixture into a pan and heat it over medium high heat until simmering. Lower heat to a low simmer and add the 2 teaspoons of tomato paste, mashing and combining well into the mixture. Let simmer for 5 minutes while stirring often. Once the sauce has thickened, remove from heat.

4 To prepare the coconut dip, whisk together mayo, coconut cream, lemon juice, onion and garlic powder, chives, dill and salt to taste until smooth. Remove the wings from the oven and place in a large mixing bowl. Coat thoroughly in sweet and spicy sauce. Serve alongside celery and dip in coconut sauce.

PALEO MAYONNAISE INGREDIENTS:

- 1 large whole egg, preferably pasture-raised
- 2 tsp. fresh lemon juice
- 2 tsp. spicy brown mustard
- 1/4 tsp. salt
- 3/4 cup avocado oil if preferred

DIRECTIONS:

1 In a tall container like a deep mason jar, add the egg, lemon juice, mustard, salt, followed by the avocado oil last.

2 Put your immersion blender down to the bottom of the container before turning on. Set it to high and blend for about 30 seconds before slowly lifting it to the surface of the mixture and moving up and down. Blend for another 20 seconds or so or until completely creamy.

SWEET + STICKY CHICKEN WINGS

PREP
5
MINUTES

MARINATE
1-8
HOURS

COOK
25
MINUTES

TOTAL
30
MINUTES

SERVES
4

If you're looking for the perfect game day appetizer, look no further! These sticky wings feed a crowd with an Asian-inspired sauce that is sweet, savory and spicy.

Starting with high-quality pasture-raised wings makes all the difference, delivering rich chicken flavor without any added antibiotics or hormones.

INGREDIENTS:

- 2 lbs. chicken wings
- 1/3 cup coconut aminos
- 2 Tbsp. coconut sugar
- 1 Tbsp. sesame oil
- 1 Tbsp. lime juice
- 1/4 tsp. cayenne pepper
- 1/4 tsp. garlic powder
- 1/4 cup green onions, chopped
- 1 Tbsp. sesame seeds for serving

EQUIPMENT:

- Mixing bowl
- Parchment paper
- Medium baking sheet
- Basting brush

DIRECTIONS:

1 Blot wings dry with paper towel. In a medium mixing bowl, whisk together coconut aminos, coconut sugar, lime juice, sesame oil, cayenne pepper, and garlic powder. Reserve 2 tablespoons of sauce and set aside. Add chicken wings to mixing bowl with sauce and toss to coat. Cover and refrigerate for 1-8 hours.

2 Preheat oven to 425°F and line a medium baking sheet with parchment paper. Place chicken wings onto prepared baking sheet. Bake for 20 minutes. Brush wings with remaining sauce and return to oven. Turn oven to broil and broil for 3-5 minutes to crisp skin. Remove from oven and sprinkle with sesame seeds and green onions. Serve hot.

LATIN ROASTED HALF CHICKEN

PREP
10
MINUTES

COOK
45
MINUTES

TOTAL
55
MINUTES

SERVES
2

If you love the Latin flavors at Brazilian restaurants, then this easy half-roasted chicken recipe will help you bring that flavor to the comfort of your own kitchen! The sauce is super versatile and can be used on fish, steak or even roasted vegetables. It's especially delicious during the summer months to jazz up recipes using fresh ingredients.

INGREDIENTS:

- 1 - 32oz half chicken
- 2 Tbsp. butter, softened
- 1 tsp. chili powder
- 1/8 tsp. sea salt

For Chimichurri Sauce:

- 1/2 cup olive oil
- 2 Tbsp. fresh lime juice
- 1/2 cup flat leaf parsley
- 1/2 cup cilantro
- 1/2 tsp. dried oregano

- 2 cloves garlic
- 1 shallot
- 1/4 tsp. sea salt
- 1/4 tsp. chili flakes

EQUIPMENT:

- 10-inch cast iron pan
- Food processor

DIRECTIONS:

1 Preheat oven to 400°F. Blot chicken dry with paper towel and place into a 10 inch oven safe dish or cast iron pan. Rub 1 tablespoon of butter under skin and 1 tablespoon on top of skin to coat legs, wings and body. Season with chili powder and sea salt. Roast for 20 minutes.

2 While chicken roasts, combine ingredients for chimichurri sauce in a food processor and pulse until just slightly chunky. Pour into a small bowl.

3 Carefully remove pan from oven and drizzle 2-3 tablespoons of chimichurri sauce over chicken. Return to oven for an additional 20-25 minutes until internal temperature reaches 165°F. Rest chicken 10 minutes before carving. Serve with remaining chimichurri sauce.

LEMON HERB ROASTED CHICKEN WITH ROOT VEGETABLES

PREP
15
MINUTES

COOK
65
MINUTES

TOTAL
2
HOURS

SERVES
4

This classic lemon herb roasted chicken is a complete meal with hearty root vegetables to keep you full. Fragrant herbs like rosemary, garlic and marjoram are complemented with the brightness of lemon zest all tied together with grass fed butter. The lemon-herb infused butter is slathered onto chicken skin, under the skin, and in the cavity adding flavor throughout and helping to crisp the skin. Any leftovers can be shredded and used in chicken soup, salads, or tacos.

INGREDIENTS:

- 1 (4-5 lb.) whole chicken
- 1/2 cup softened unsalted butter
- 1 Tbsp. lemon zest
- 1 tsp. dried marjoram
- 1 tsp. dried thyme
- 1/4 tsp. garlic powder
- 1 tsp. sea salt
- 1/2 tsp. cracked black pepper

- 2 sprigs fresh rosemary
- 1 lemon, halved
- 3 cups peeled/chopped turnips
- 2 cups chopped carrots
- 1 cup chopped red onion

EQUIPMENT:

- Dutch oven or heavy pan

DIRECTIONS:

1 Preheat oven to 425°F. Scatter chopped turnips, carrots and red onion in the bottom of a heavy pan or Dutch oven. Rinse chicken thoroughly under cool water and pat dry with paper towel on skin and in cavity.

2 Place chicken on top of vegetables. Stir together softened butter, thyme, marjoram, lemon zest, garlic powder, sea salt and black pepper. Rub butter under skin on breasts and all over the top of skin. Add a large chunk of butter to the cavity along with rosemary sprig and half of the lemon.

3 Tuck wings behind chicken and tie legs together. Place in oven on middle rack. Roast for 20 minutes.

4 Reduce heat to 375°F and continue to roast for 45 minutes-1 hour or until a meat thermometer inserted into chicken thigh reads 165°F.

5 Remove from oven and rest chicken for 15-20 minutes before slicing.

ROASTED JAMAICAN JERK CHICKEN

PREP
20
MINUTES

COOK
50
MINUTES

TOTAL
75
MINUTES

SERVES
4

P CERTIFIED PALEO · CERTIFIED PALEO
K KETO FRIENDLY · KETO FRIENDLY
GLUTEN FREE · GLUTEN FREE
DAIRY FREE · DAIRY FREE

This fragrant roasted jerk chicken has something for everyone, utilizing all the best parts of the chicken—from legs to thighs! Chicken pieces are coated in a thick marinade that's sweet and savory with warm spices like cinnamon, allspice, and ginger balanced with sweet coconut sugar. To balance the rich flavor of the jerk chicken is an avocado salsa fresca with fresh lime juice and cherry tomatoes. It's like a trip to the islands without leaving home!

INGREDIENTS:

- 1 whole chicken, broken into 8 pieces

  For Jerk Seasoning:

- 1/4 cup olive oil
- 1 Tbsp. coconut sugar
- 1 tsp. paprika
- 1 tsp. dried thyme
- 1/2 tsp. garlic powder
- 1/4 tsp. onion powder
- 1/2 tsp. ground allspice
- 1/2 tsp. ground ginger
- 1/4 tsp. cayenne pepper
- 1/8 tsp. cracked black pepper
- 1 tsp. sea salt

  For Avocado Salsa:

- 1 large ripe avocado, peeled/diced
- 1 cup halved cherry tomatoes
- 1/4 cup red onion
- 2 Tbsp. lime juice
- 2 Tbsp. chopped cilantro
- 1 Tbsp. thinly sliced jalapeño
- 1/2 tsp. sea salt

EQUIPMENT:

- Roasting pan

DIRECTIONS:

1 Preheat oven to 375°F. Stir together ingredients for jerk seasoning to form a thick paste. Coat chicken pieces with mixture on all sides. Place on a medium baking sheet.

2 Roast chicken for 45-50 minutes. Turn the oven to broil for the last 3-5 minutes.

3 While chicken is roasting, make salsa by combining all ingredients in a small bowl and stirring gently. Serve jerk chicken pieces with avocado salsa.

ROASTED WHOLE CHICKEN

PREP
10
MINUTES

COOK
90
MINUTES

TOTAL
100
MINUTES

SERVES
4

Enjoy rotisserie chicken flavor in under 2 hours! This whole roasted chicken is full of buttery herb flavor with crispy skin and juicy, tender meat. A 5 pound chicken will serve 4 people. To turn this recipe into a complete meal, roast the chicken on top of chopped sweet potato and onion for a touch of sweetness and vibrant color that pair perfectly with the herbed butter. If you want more vegetables, feel free to add carrots, parsnips, celery, or fennel for a delicious meal.

TIP! *Check the temperature of chicken by inserting a meat thermometer into the thickest part of the thigh without touching the bone. Omit herbed butter to make this recipe Paleo friendly.*

INGREDIENTS:

- 1 (5 lb.) whole chicken (neck and giblets removed)
- 1 lb. sweet potatoes, cubed
- 1 red onion, coarsely chopped
- 1 lemon, halved
- 2 sprigs fresh rosemary (divided)
- 4 sprigs fresh thyme (divided)

    For Herbed Butter:

- 1/3 cup unsalted grass fed butter, softened

- 2 cloves garlic, minced
- 1 tsp. dried thyme
- 1/2 tsp. dried marjoram
- 1 tsp. sea salt
- 1/2 tsp. black pepper

EQUIPMENT:

- Small mixing bowl
- 5 quart dutch oven or roasting pan

DIRECTIONS:

1 Preheat oven to 425°F. Place chicken on a cutting board and pat dry with paper towel. Add sweet potato, onion and half of fresh herbs to a roasting pan or dutch oven.

2 Stir together ingredients for herbed butter in a small mixing bowl until thoroughly combined. Cover chicken skin, under skin and inside cavity with herbed butter. Place 1/2 of the lemon, 1 sprig of rosemary and 2 sprigs of thyme inside the cavity. Tie legs together with kitchen twine (optional).

3 Place chicken on top of vegetables in pot and tuck wings behind the chicken. Add remaining lemon half. On the lowest rack in oven, roast for 1 1/2 hours or until internal temperature reaches 170°F. Remove pot from oven and rest at room temperature for 20 minutes before slicing.

100% GRASS FED BEEF

WHY GRASS FINISHED MATTERS

Did you know a lot of "grass fed" beef is finished on grains? That's why all Wild Pastures beef is grass fed and finished. Our cattle are never fed grain or given antibiotics or hormones. Our cattle eat grass... that's it!

Our cattle are never confined to a feedlot or static plot of pasture. Instead, they are rotationally grazed. Rotational grazing helps preserve and restore the health of the land while providing a more nutrient-rich, natural diet for cattle.

Wild Pastures livestock are raised in the USA. Most other grass fed beef is imported. As long as it is packaged in America, it can be labeled as American beef. We only work with highly ethical family farmers right here on healthy American soil.

BREAKFAST SAUSAGE BOWL

PREP
5
MINUTES

COOK
26
MINUTES

TOTAL
31
MINUTES

SERVES
2

This breakfast bowl will keep you satisfied with plenty of protein, fat and fiber. Hearty sweet potatoes add staying power and beta-carotene while kale delivers vitamin K. Herby pre-seasoned breakfast sausage makes prep work a breeze, perfect for busy mornings.

INGREDIENTS:

- 1/2 lb. beef breakfast sausage
- 2 cups chopped kale
- 1 Tbsp. olive oil
- 2 cups chopped sweet potato
- 2 eggs
- 1 Tbsp. minced chives
- Sea salt and black pepper to taste

EQUIPMENT:

- Medium skillet

DIRECTIONS:

1 Heat breakfast sausage over medium heat in a medium skillet. Use a spatula to break up into small pieces. Cook 8 minutes, stirring regularly. Add chopped kale and stir. Continue to cook 3 minutes.

2 While breakfast sausage cooks, heat olive oil in a separate medium skillet. Add sweet potatoes and cook for 12-15 minutes, until potatoes are cooked through. Stir in chives.

3 Add cooked breakfast sausage and sweet potatoes to two serving bowls. Top each with 2 fried eggs and season with salt and pepper. Enjoy hot.

BEEF CHORIZO + SPINACH FRITTATA

PREP
10
MINUTES

COOK
40
MINUTES

TOTAL
60
MINUTES

SERVES
8

P CERTIFIED PALEO · CERTIFIED PALEO

K KETO FRIENDLY · KETO FRIENDLY

GLUTEN FREE · GLUTEN FREE

DAIRY FREE · DAIRY FREE

Spicy chorizo sausage adds southwest flavor to this 6 ingredient frittata that cooks up in under an hour! It is full of protein from eggs and chorizo and makes enough servings to feed a crowd or refrigerate to have on hand during the week.

INGREDIENTS:

- 1 lb. beef chorizo sausage

- 4 cups fresh spinach

- 10 large eggs

- 1/3 cup unsweetened almond or coconut milk

- 1/2 tsp. sea salt

- 1/3 cup fresh cilantro for serving

- 1 Tbsp. of olive oil

EQUIPMENT:

- 9-inch cast iron pan

DIRECTIONS:

1 Preheat oven to 350°F. Whisk together eggs, almond milk and sea salt in a large mixing bowl.

2 Lightly grease a 9-inch cast iron pan with olive oil and add chorizo. Heat on stovetop over medium heat. Cook for 4-5 minutes using a spatula to break up chorizo into small pieces. Stir in spinach and continue to cook for 4 minutes longer to wilt spinach. Turn heat off.

3 Pour egg mixture over chorizo and transfer to oven. Bake 25-30 minutes or until eggs are cooked through.

4 Cool for 10 minutes at room temperature before slicing. Enjoy topped with fresh cilantro.

SWEET POTATO + CHORIZO FRITTERS

PREP
5
MINUTES

COOK
26
MINUTES

TOTAL
31
MINUTES

SERVES
2

These sweet and savory breakfast fritters are a great meal prep option to have on hand for busy mornings. They're loaded with fiber, protein and good-for-you fats. The zesty chorizo beef sausage adds loads of flavor and only 5 ingredients total!

INGREDIENTS:

- 1/2 lb. beef chorizo sausage
- 1 cup tightly packed peeled, grated sweet potato
- 1 large egg
- 2 Tbsp. blanched almond flour
- 2 Tbsp. chopped cilantro
- Oil of your preference

EQUIPMENT:

- Medium skillet
- Medium mixing bowl

DIRECTIONS:

1 Combine chorizo, sweet potato, egg, almond flour and cilantro in a medium mixing bowl and stir well to combine.

2 Scoop 1/3 cup of mixture and use hands to form into a small patty. Repeat with remaining mixture to create 6-7 fritters.

3 Heat oil in a medium pan over medium heat for 2 minutes. Add 3-4 fritters to pan and cook for 3 minutes on each side.

4 Transfer cooked fritters to a plate. Repeat with remaining fritters. Enjoy hot.

ONE POT BEEF STEW

PREP
10
MINUTES

COOK
4.25
HOURS

TOTAL
4.5
HOURS

SERVES
6-8

This one-pot beef stew is a hearty Paleo twist on the age old favorite. Using tried and true ingredients along with Paleo staples like ghee, coconut aminos and arrowroot flour, it's a wholesome dish without inflammatory ingredients.

Substituting for potatoes are celery, onion and carrots. Sweet potatoes or parsnips can also be added. Once the stew is prepared it can be refrigerated in an airtight container up to one week for a weeknight heat-and-eat meal.

INGREDIENTS:

- 2 lbs. beef stew meat
- 2 Tbsp. ghee
- 1 small sweet white onion, chopped
- 2 cups celery, coarsely chopped
- 4 medium carrots, coarsely chopped
- 2 garlic cloves, minced
- 4 cups beef stock
- 1/2 cup tomato sauce
- 2 Tbsp. coconut aminos
- 1 tsp. dried oregano
- 2 bay leaves
- 2 Tbsp. arrowroot flour
- 1/2 tsp. sea salt
- 1/2 tsp. black pepper

EQUIPMENT:

- 5 quart dutch oven
- Whisk

DIRECTIONS:

1 Heat ghee in a 5 quart dutch oven over medium-high heat for 2-3 minutes. Add beef stew meat and brown on all sides for 7 minutes, stirring occasionally.

2 Add remaining ingredients except arrowroot flour and bring to a boil. Reduce heat to low. Cover and simmer for 4 hours or until beef is fall apart tender.

3 Remove 1 cup of broth from pot and combine with arrowroot powder, whisking together. Pour mixture back into pot and stir well. Cook 5 minutes longer to allow arrowroot flour to thicken the broth. Ladle into bowls and serve hot.

PRESSURE COOKER JAMAICAN BEEF STEW

PREP
10
MINUTES

COOK
48
MINUTES

TOTAL
58
MINUTES

SERVES
4

Give your traditional beef stew an upgrade with this aromatic Jamaican stew full of fragrant spices like allspice and garlic. Coconut sugar adds a touch of sweetness that balances the spicy heat of the stew. Chunks of tender beef add staying power along with carrots and bell pepper. Serve alongside pan-fried plantains for an island feast that's Paleo approved! Best of all, this version is made in a pressure cooker for a stew that's ready in an hour.

INGREDIENTS:

- 1 lb. beef stew meat
- 1 Tbsp. ghee
- 1 1/2 cups beef stock
- 2 sprigs fresh thyme
- 1 cup chopped white onion
- 1 cup chopped green bell pepper
- 1 cup peeled/chopped carrots
- 1/2 cup tomato sauce
- 2 Tbsp. tomato paste
- 2 Tbsp. coconut aminos

- 1 Tbsp. Paleo compliant hot sauce
- 1/4 tsp. ground allspice
- 1/4 tsp. garlic powder
- 1 Tbsp. coconut sugar
- 2 dried bay leaves
- 1/2 tsp. sea salt
- 1/4 tsp. cracked black pepper

EQUIPMENT:

- Instant pot/pressure cooker

DIRECTIONS:

1 Press sauté setting on instant pot and melt ghee. Blot beef stew meat with paper towel to remove excess moisture. Once ghee is shimmering, add beef and brown for 8 minutes, stirring after 4 minutes. Press cancel.

2 Stir in beef stock and add sprigs of thyme. Lock lid and close vent valve. Press manual for 25 minutes. When timer goes off, allow pressure cooker to naturally release, then open vent valve and allow remaining pressure to release.

3 Remove lid and add carrots, onion, bell pepper, tomato paste, tomato sauce and all remaining ingredients. Stir well. Lock lid and close vent valve. Press manual setting to 15 minutes. When timer goes off allow pressure to release before opening vent valve and removing lid. Ladle into bowls and serve hot.

BEEF BONE BROTH ZUCCHINI RAMEN

PREP
10
MINUTES

COOK
12
MINUTES

TOTAL
22
MINUTES

SERVES
2

This gut-healing bone broth ramen is Paleo-friendly using zucchini noodles instead of traditional ramen noodles. Bone broth provides amino acids that help support healthy gut lining as well as improve skin and joint elasticity. The broth is simmered with ginger, garlic, coconut aminos and tangy lime juice before being poured over raw veggies.

This soup is especially comforting in cooler months to help support the immune system and warm you from the inside out!

INGREDIENTS:

- 4 cups beef bone broth
- 1 tsp. minced garlic
- 1 Tbsp. grated ginger
- 3 fresh lime juice
- 2 Tbsp. coconut aminos
- 1/2 tsp. sea salt
- 1 medium zucchini, spiral sliced or peeled using a julienne peeler
- 1/2 cup shredded carrots

- 1 cup sliced shiitake mushrooms
- 1/2 cup basil leaves
- 1/4 cup chopped green onion
- 1 soft boiled egg, sliced in half lengthwise

EQUIPMENT:

- Spiralizer/julienne peeler
- Saucepan

DIRECTIONS:

1 Heat bone broth, coconut aminos, lime juice, garlic, ginger and sea salt over medium-high heat in a saucepan until boiling about 6-7 minutes. Reduce heat to low and simmer for 5 minutes.

2 Arrange zucchini noodles, shiitake mushrooms and shredded carrots in 2 serving bowls and ladle hot bone broth on top.

3 Top each bowl with basil leaves, green onion and a half of a soft boiled egg. Enjoy hot.

PRESSURE COOKER BRISKET CHILI

PREP
10
MINUTES

COOK
83
MINUTES

TOTAL
93
MINUTES

SERVES
4

CERTIFIED PALEO · CERTIFIED PALEO
P

KETO FRIENDLY · KETO FRIENDLY
K

GLUTEN FREE · GLUTEN FREE

DAIRY FREE · DAIRY FREE

This smoky Paleo brisket chili is a recipe that is any beef lover's go-to. It's perfect for game days and cold autumn evenings when a hot bowl of hearty chili is a must have. Plenty of antioxidant-rich veggies balance this high-protein recipe that pressure cooks in under 2 hours.

INGREDIENTS:

- 2 1/2 lbs. grass fed beef brisket
- 6 oz. tomato paste
- 1 cup beef stock
- 1 cup chopped celery
- 1 cup chopped carrots
- 1 cup chopped bell pepper
- 1 cup chopped white onion
- 15 oz. can fire roasted tomatoes
- 1/4 cup coconut aminos
- 2 Tbsp. ground cumin

- 1 Tbsp. dried oregano
- 2 tsp. smoked paprika
- 1 tsp. garlic powder
- 1/2 tsp. red pepper flakes
- 1 tsp. sea salt
- 1/2 cup cilantro for serving
- 1/4 cup pumpkin seeds for garnish

EQUIPMENT:

- Instant pot/pressure cooker

DIRECTIONS:

1 Turn pressure cooker to sauté setting. Slice beef into 5 chunks and blot dry with paper towel. Place beef in instant pot and sauté for 8 minutes, turning after 4 minutes to brown meat. Press cancel.

2 Pour in beef stock. Secure lid and close vent cap. Press meat/chicken setting or Manual for 1 hour.

3 Once timer goes off, allow pot to depressurize then open vent valve to release any remaining pressure. Remove lid and place beef on cutting board. Shred well with 2 forks and return to pot.

4 Add tomatoes, tomato paste, coconut aminos, smoked paprika, garlic powder, oregano, cumin, sea salt and red pepper flakes to pot and stir. Stir in carrots, bell pepper, onion and celery. Return lid and lock. Press stew/soup setting for 15 minutes and close pressure valve.

5 Allow pot to depressurize before removing lid. Ladle chili into bowls and serve topped with cilantro and a sprinkle of pumpkin seeds.

BRAISED BEEF RAGU

PREP
10
MINUTES

COOK
4.5
HOURS

TOTAL
5
HOURS

SERVES
6-8

If you're looking for a pasta sauce that tastes like old world Italian cooking, look no further than this braised beef ragu. Like the name says, beef is slow-cooked in herbs and tomatoes until fall-apart tender. This hearty sauce begs to be smothered over veggie noodles, cauliflower polenta or spooned over baked sweet potatoes.

We opted to let the beef stand on its own in this recipe, but you can also add finely chopped vegetables like carrots, onion and celery if you would like to amp up the vegetable content. Any leftovers can be frozen for up to 4 months in an airtight container.

NOTE! *For those following strict Paleo or Whole30, coconut sugar and red wine can be omitted.*

INGREDIENTS:

- 24 oz. chuck roast
- 1 Tbsp. ghee
- 1 tsp. garlic, minced
- 1 (28 oz) can crushed tomatoes
- 1 cup beef stock
- 1 tsp. dried oregano
- 1 sprig rosemary
- 2-3 sprigs thyme

- 1/4 cup dry red wine
- 1 Tbsp. coconut sugar
- 2 tsp. sea salt
- 1/2 cup fresh basil for serving

EQUIPMENT:

- Medium cast iron skillet
- 5 quart dutch oven or stock pot

DIRECTIONS:

1 Pat chuck roast dry with paper towel. Heat a medium cast iron skillet over medium-high heat. Add ghee. When ghee is melted and shimmering, add chuck and sear 4-5 minutes each side. Turn off heat. Add garlic to pan and allow to cook 30 seconds.

2 Transfer chuck roast to a large pot or dutch oven over medium heat. Immediately pour garlic and beef drippings over beef. Add beef stock, tomatoes, sprig of rosemar, thyme and oregano. Bring to a boil. Reduce heat to simmer. Cover with lid slightly cracked and simmer 4 hours or until beef easily falls apart.

3 Remove rosemary and thyme sprigs. Shred beef with 2 forks and return to pot. Add red wine, salt, and coconut sugar. Cook uncovered an additional 30 minutes, taste and adjust if necessary. Serve over veggie noodles and garnish with fresh basil.

CHUCK ROAST ITALIAN BEEF

PREP
5
MINUTES

COOK
90
MINUTES

TOTAL
95
MINUTES

SERVES
4

P — CERTIFIED PALEO
K — KETO FRIENDLY
GLUTEN FREE
DAIRY FREE

If you're short on time but want a comfort food meal with cooked all day, fall apart goodness, this is the recipe for you. Chuck roast is pressure cooked in a tangy, herb liquid and in just over an hour, it shreds easily. It's perfect for enjoying on its own with spicy giardiniera or on a paleo compliant sub roll with a generous drizzle of au jus.

INGREDIENTS:

- 3 lb. chuck roast
- 1 Tbsp. avocado oil
- 1 cup beef stock
- 1/2 cup banana pepper rings with juice
- 2 Tbsp. coconut aminos
- 2 dried bay leaves
- 1 Tbsp. minced garlic
- 2 tsp. dried basil

- 2 tsp. dried oregano
- 1/2 tsp. onion powder
- 1 tsp. sea salt
- 1/2 tsp. black pepper
- Giardiniera or spicy pickled vegetables, for serving

EQUIPMENT:

- Instant pot/pressure cooker

DIRECTIONS:

1 Heat avocado oil in an instant pot on sauté setting. Blot chuck roast dry with paper towel and season on both sides with sea salt and black pepper. Brown chuck roast on both sides for 4 minutes. If chuck is too large to fit in pot, slice into 2-3 pieces.

2 Add remaining ingredients to instant pot except giardiniera. Secure lid and close vent valve. Press manual setting for 1 hour and 20 minutes.

3 When timer goes off, allow pressure to release for 5 minutes. Open vent valve and release any additional pressure.Remove lid and pull out chuck roast pieces. Shred beef using two forks. Add beef back into the pressure cooker and toss in juices. Serve hot on it's own or on a paleo friendly sub roll topped with giardiniera.

HORSERADISH CRUSTED FILET MIGNON

PREP
10
MINUTES

COOK
10
MINUTES

TOTAL
35
MINUTES

SERVES
2

Enjoy steakhouse flavor right at home with this Paleo-friendly horseradish crusted filet mignon! Pork rinds add crispy texture without the use of breadcrumbs, something you won't find offered at most steakhouses. This unique swap keeps the recipe low in carbs without sacrificing flavor.

INGREDIENTS:

- 2 (6-8oz) beef filet mignon
- 1 Tbsp. avocado oil
- 1/2 tsp. sea salt
- 1/8 tsp. cracked black pepper

    For Horseradish Sauce:

- 1 cup plain pork rinds
- 2 Tbsp. grated horseradish
- 2 tsp. Paleo mayonnaise
- 1 tsp. Dijon mustard

EQUIPMENT:

- Cast iron skillet

DIRECTIONS:

1 Set steaks out at room temperature for 10 minutes. Heat oven to broil on high heat.

2 Heat a cast iron skillet over medium-high heat and lightly grease with avocado oil. Let the skillet heat for 3-4 minutes. While pan heats, season steaks on both sides with salt and pepper.

3 Place steaks in pan and sear for 2 minutes. Turn steaks over and spoon horseradish mixture on top.

4 Transfer to oven and broil for 4-5 minutes, until crust is golden brown. Rest steak at room temperature for 5 minutes before serving.

FLANK STEAK STIR FRY

PREP
10
MINUTES

COOK
20
MINUTES

TOTAL
30
MINUTES

SERVES
4

This quick and easy Asian dinner curbs the craving for takeout with strips of flank steak and veggies all tossed in a sweet and savory stir fry sauce! Serve over cauliflower rice or zucchini noodles if desired.

INGREDIENTS:

- 1 lb. flank steak, sliced to 1/4 inch thick
- 1/2 cup coconut aminos
- 3 Tbsp. toasted sesame oil (divided)
- 1 Tbsp. lime juice
- 2 tsp. arrowroot flour
- 1 tsp. coconut sugar
- 1/2 tsp. minced garlic
- 1/4 tsp. ground ginger
- 2 cups broccoli florets
- 1/2 cup thinly sliced carrots
- 1/2 cup sliced sweet white onion
- 1 tsp. toasted sesame seeds

EQUIPMENT:

- Cast iron skillet

DIRECTIONS:

1 Whisk together coconut aminos, 2 tablespoons sesame oil, lime juice, garlic, ginger, arrowroot flour and coconut sugar in a small bowl. Set aside.

2 Heat 1 tablespoon sesame oil over medium-high heat in a cast iron skillet for 2 minutes. Blot sliced steak with paper towel and add to skillet. Brown for 3 minutes on each side.

3 Add broccoli, carrots and onion to skillet and pour sauce on top. Gently stir to coat. Bring to a simmer and reduce heat to medium.

4 Simmer for 6-8 minutes longer, until sauce has thickened slightly. Serve hot topped with sesame seeds.

FLAT IRON STEAK BURRITO BOWL

PREP
10
MINUTES

COOK
11
MINUTES

TOTAL
21
MINUTES

SERVES
2

P — CERTIFIED PALEO
K — KETO FRIENDLY
GLUTEN FREE
DAIRY FREE

Skip the tortilla and enjoy this protein-packed steak burrito bowl instead. Complete with vitamin-C rich cauliflower rice and a mix of raw and sauteed vegetables, this Mexican style bowl is a Paleo-approved alternative to fast food!

INGREDIENTS:

- 1/2 lb. flat iron steak, thinly sliced
- 1 tsp. olive oil + extra for cooking
- 1 Tbsp. lime juice
- 1 tsp. ground cumin
- 1/2 tsp. chili powder
- 1/2 tsp. sea salt
- 1/8 tsp. onion powder
- 1 cup thinly sliced bell pepper
- 2 cups cauliflower rice

- 1 cup sliced lettuce
- 1/2 cup chopped red onion
- 1/2 cup sliced avocado
- 1/2 cup salsa or pico de gallo
- 2 Tbsp. fresh cilantro

EQUIPMENT:

- Cast iron skillet

DIRECTIONS:

1 Combine 1 teaspoon olive oil, lime juice, cumin, chili powder, onion powder and sea salt in a medium mixing bowl and stir to combine. Add steak and toss to coat.

2 Lightly grease a large cast iron skillet with olive oil. Heat over medium-high heat for 2 minutes. Add steak and sear for 2-3 minutes on each side.

3 Transfer steak to a plate and reduce heat to medium. Add bell peppers and 1 teaspoon of olive oil. Sauté for 5 minutes stirring occasionally.

4 Divide cauliflower rice, lettuce and red onion between 2 bowls and add steak and sautéed bell peppers. Top with avocado, salsa and fresh cilantro.

ITALIAN BEEF SAUSAGE TUSCAN SOUP

PREP
10
MINUTES

COOK
30
MINUTES

TOTAL
40
MINUTES

SERVES
4

You don't need a lot of ingredients to make a satisfying and delicious soup. This 8-ingredient recipe is full of robust herb flavor thanks to Italian seasoned grass fed beef, for a soup that's high in protein and antioxidants rich vegetables.

INGREDIENTS:

- 1 lb. Italian seasoned ground beef sausage
- 1 Tbsp. ghee
- 1/2 cup chopped sweet white onion
- 1 cup chopped celery
- 4 cups beef stock
- 1 (15 oz) can diced tomatoes
- 2 cups chopped kale
- 1/2 cup fresh basil for topping
- Sea salt, to taste

EQUIPMENT:

- Dutch oven or heavy pot

DIRECTIONS:

1 Heat ghee over medium heat in a 4 quart Dutch oven or heavy pot. Add celery and onion and sauté for 5 minutes.

2 Move vegetables to the side of pot and add Italian beef sausage. Use a wooden spatula to break up sausage into small pieces. Cook for 8 minutes, stirring occasionally.

3 Add tomatoes and beef stock to pot and bring to a boil. Reduce heat to medium-low and simmer for 10-15 minutes.

4 Stir in sea salt and kale and cook 2 minutes longer to wilt kale. Ladle into bowls and enjoy hot topped with chopped basil.

ITALIAN STUFFED PEPPERS

PREP
10
MINUTES

COOK
40
MINUTES

TOTAL
55
MINUTES

SERVES
3-4

These Paleo stuffed peppers ditch the rice and load up on vitamin D rich mushrooms instead. Italian seasoned ground beef adds plenty of herb flavor from fennel, basil, and oregano. Best of all, it can be easily reheated and is Keto friendly.

INGREDIENTS:

- 1 lb. Italian ground beef sausage
- 3 medium bell peppers
- 1 1/2 cups chopped white button mushrooms
- 1/2 cup chopped sweet white onion
- 1/3 cup tomato paste
- 1/4 cup water
- Oil of your preference

- 1/4 tsp. sea salt
- 1/4 cup chopped basil or parsley

EQUIPMENT:

- 9x13 baking dish
- Skillet
- Parchment paper

DIRECTIONS:

1 Preheat oven to 400°F and line a 9x13 baking dish with parchment paper. Slice peppers in half lengthwise to create 6 halves. Remove seeds and place peppers in baking dish cut side down. Bake for 15 minutes.

2 In the meantime, heat oil over medium heat in a skillet and add mushrooms and onions. Sauté for 6-7 minutes. Transfer sautéed vegetables to a bowl.

3 Add ground Italian beef sausage to hot pan and brown for 6 minutes, breaking into small pieces with a spatula. Drain excess grease from pan.

4 Add sautéed vegetables to pan with beef and stir in tomato paste, sea salt, and water. Simmer for 2 minutes.

5 Turn bell peppers so the cut side is facing up. Spoon beef mixture into peppers. Return to oven for 10-15 minutes.

6 Remove from the oven and cool for 5 minutes. Serve hot topped with chopped parsley or basil.

HERB BUTTER NY STRIP STEAK

PREP
5
MINUTES

COOK
15
MINUTES

TOTAL
20
MINUTES

SERVES
2

Date night at home is a cinch with this grass fed NY strip steak dinner complete with an herb butter and broccolini. Best of all, this dish is ready for the table in 20 minutes flat! A fancy feast has never been this simple.

INGREDIENTS:

- 2-8 oz. NY strip steaks
- 1 tsp. olive oil
- 2 Tbsp. unsalted butter, at room temperature (divided)
- 1/4 tsp. chopped rosemary leaves
- 1/4 tsp. fresh thyme leaves
- 1/4 tsp. dried oregano
- 1/4 tsp. minced garlic
- 1/4 tsp. black pepper
- 1/2 tsp. sea salt
- 6 broccolini stalks

EQUIPMENT:

- Small bowl
- Medium skillet
- Tongs

DIRECTIONS:

1 Blot steaks dry using paper towel. Season with salt and pepper. In a small bowl, use a fork to mash butter, rosemary, thyme, oregano and garlic together. Set aside

2 Heat olive oil in a medium skillet over medium-high heat for 2 minutes. Place steaks on hot skillet and sear for 3-4 minutes (for medium). Flip steaks using tongs and place half of butter mixture on top of each steak. Sear an additional 3-4 minutes. Transfer steaks to a plate to rest.

3 Reduce heat to medium and add broccolini and remaining herb butter to pan. Cover and cook 5 minutes. Serve broccolini immediately alongside steaks.

MONGOLIAN BEEF AND CHARRED BROCCOLINI

PREP
5
MINUTES

COOK
16
MINUTES

TOTAL
21
MINUTES

SERVES
2

Strip steaks are full of beefy flavor with plenty of marbling throughout which helps create a juicy flavor. This cut is tender and perfect for quick cooking over high heat. Use sirloin or ribeye. The rich sauce is made using only 4 ingredients with a sweet and savory flavor. To bulk up the recipe, serve over jasmine rice or riced cauliflower for Paleo.

INGREDIENTS:

- 1 lb. NY strip steaks, thinly sliced
- 1 Tbsp. gluten-free flour (brown rice, arrowroot, cassava)
- 2 Tbsp. avocado oil (divided)
- 1 Tbsp. coconut sugar
- 1/3 cup coconut aminos
- 1 tsp. minced garlic
- 1/2 tsp. grated ginger
- 8 oz. broccolini
- 1/3 cup chopped green onion
- 1 tsp. sesame seeds

EQUIPMENT:

- Small bowl
- Medium cast iron pan
- Medium mixing bowl

DIRECTIONS:

1 Stir together coconut aminos, coconut sugar, garlic and ginger in a small bowl. Set aside.

2 Heat 1 tablespoon of avocado oil in a medium cast iron skillet over medium-high heat for 3 minutes. Add broccolini and cook 2 minutes. Use tongs to turn and cook an additional 2 minutes. Transfer broccolini to serving plate.

3 In a medium mixing bowl, use hands to toss strips of steak in flour to coat.

4 Wipe cast iron skillet clean with a paper towel. Add 1 tablespoon of avocado oil to skillet over medium-high heat and heat for 2 minutes. Add steak strips and cook for 4-5 minutes to brown, stirring occasionally. Reduce heat to medium. Pour in sauce and stir gently. Cook an additional 2 minutes. Serve steak over broccolini garnished with chopped green onion and sesame seeds.

PERFECT STEAK

PREP
5
MINUTES

COOK
8
MINUTES

TOTAL
13
MINUTES

SERVES
2

You don't need fancy ingredients to serve mouthwatering, tender steak with a crisp crust on the outside and tender pink in the center.

With a few crucial tips, you'll be on your way to foolproof steak every time. Simply make sure you use a cast iron pan, blot steaks dry before searing, season well, baste with butter and herbs, and let rest for 5 minutes after cooking. If you follow these simple rules, you'll cook the perfect steak every time.

INGREDIENTS:

- 2 NY strip steaks
- 1/2 tsp. sea salt
- 1/4 tsp. black pepper
- 1 Tbsp. avocado oil or olive oil
- 2 Tbsp. butter
- 4 cloves garlic, crushed
- 2 sprigs thyme
- 1 small sprig rosemary

EQUIPMENT:

- Medium cast iron pan
- Tongs

DIRECTIONS:

1 Heat oil in a medium cast iron pan over medium-high heat for 3-5 minutes or until oil is shimmering hot. Blot steaks dry with a paper towel and season on both sides with salt and pepper.

2 Place steaks on hot pan and cook 3 minutes on each side to brown. Reduce heat to medium-low and add butter, garlic, thyme and rosemary. Use an oven mitt and carefully tilt pan, rotating wrist to move the butter herb mixture around. Cook 1-2 minutes longer using a spoon to baste steaks with butter mixture.

3 Transfer steaks to a cutting board and let sit for 5 minutes. Slice steak against the grain and serve with reserved butter mixture on top.

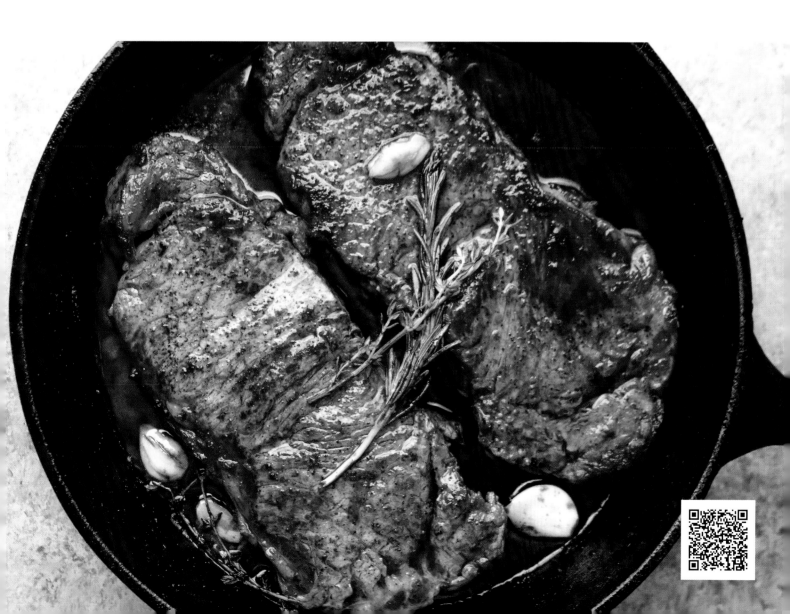

BREAKFAST BURGER

PREP
5
MINUTES

COOK
20
MINUTES

TOTAL
25
MINUTES

SERVES
4

These breakfast burgers are sure to turn anyone into a morning person! With grass fed beef seasoned like breakfast sausage then topped with a runny egg and crisp bacon, this high-protein burger is a complete meal in itself!

1 pound of beef makes 4 large burgers, perfect for serving breakfast to a group or as a weekly meal prep. The burgers can be refrigerated and reheated as needed for quick assembly on busy mornings. Serve burgers on top of grain-free buns for a complete Paleo breakfast!

INGREDIENTS:

- 1 lb. ground beef
- 2 Tbsp. pure maple syrup
- 2 tsp. dry rubbed sage
- 1/2 tsp. onion powder
- 1 tsp. black pepper
- 1/2 tsp. sea salt
- 1 Tbsp. avocado oil for cooking

    Optional toppings:
- 4 eggs

- 4 strips bacon, cooked
- 1 medium tomato, thinly sliced
- 1 cup arugula
- 4 Paleo buns

EQUIPMENT:

- Medium mixing bowl
- Medium skillet

DIRECTIONS:

1 Combine ingredients for burgers in a medium mixing bowl. Use hands to thoroughly mix.

2 Form into 4 patties. Heat avocado oil over medium heat in a medium cast iron skillet for 2 minutes. Place 1-2 patties into skillet and cook 4-5 minutes on each side. Repeat with remaining patties.

3 Cook eggs to sunny-side-up or according to your preferences. Assemble burgers on buns and top with suggested toppings. Enjoy immediately.

CUBAN PICADILLO

PREP
10
MINUTES

COOK
23
MINUTES

TOTAL
33
MINUTES

SERVES
4

Enjoy the exotic flavor of Cuban picadillo in this sweet and savory dish. Zesty tomato flavor runs throughout this dish with smoky cumin and briny olives adding depth. Raisins add complexity and sweetness as they plump in the savory sauce. Serve alongside pan-fried plantains and a scoop of cauliflower rice to round out the dish.

INGREDIENTS:

- 1 lb. ground beef
- 2 Tbsp. unsalted butter
- 1 cup chopped sweet white onion
- 1 cup chopped green bell pepper
- 2 tsp. cumin
- 2 dried bay leaves
- 1 tsp. dried oregano
- 1 tsp. minced garlic
- 1/2 tsp. sea salt
- 1 (8 oz) can no added sugar tomato sauce
- 1/3 cup beef stock or bone broth
- 1/3 cup chopped green olives
- 1/4 cup unsweetened raisins
- 1/4 cup chopped cilantro for serving
- 4 cups riced cauliflower
- 1 large ripe plantain, sliced into 1/2 inch pieces and sautéed in ghee 3 minutes on both sides

EQUIPMENT:

- Skillet

DIRECTIONS:

1 Melt butter in a medium skillet over medium heat. Add onions and bell pepper. Sauté for 7-8 minutes, stirring occasionally.

2 Move vegetables to the side of the pan and add ground beef, using a spatula to break up into pieces. Cook 5 minutes longer.

3 Stir in cumin, oregano, garlic, sea salt and stir to combine. Stir beef stock, tomato sauce, olives and raisins. Add bay leaves and reduce heat to low.

4 Simmer mixture for 10 minutes longer. Serve hot alongside riced cauliflower and plantains. Garnish with chopped cilantro.

GREEK GYRO BURGER

PREP
5
MINUTES

COOK
16
MINUTES

TOTAL
21
MINUTES

SERVES
4

Take a trip to the Mediterranean with these Greek gyro inspired burgers bursting with herb flavor. Pile them high with your favorite veggies and tangy raw feta cheese for a meal that satisfies!

For those following a strict Paleo diet, cashew or cauliflower cheese can be substituted. A smear of Paleo mayonnaise would also work. This exotic burger recipe is particularly delicious during the hot summer months for backyard entertaining!

INGREDIENTS:

- 1 lb. 80/20 ground beef
- 2 Tbsp. chopped curly parsley
- 1/2 tsp. dried oregano
- 1/2 tsp. dried dill
- 1/2 tsp. dried basil
- 1/4 tsp. onion powder
- 1 Tbsp. olive oil for cooking
- 1/2 tsp. black pepper
- 1/2 tsp. sea salt

- Chopped olives
- Sun-dried tomato
- Roasted red pepper
- Fresh basil
- Sliced red onion
- Raw feta cheese
- Paleo hamburger buns

Optional toppings:

- Sliced tomatoes
- Cucumber

EQUIPMENT:

- Medium mixing bowl
- Medium skillet

DIRECTIONS:

1 Combine ingredients for burgers in a medium mixing bowl and mix thoroughly to combine. Form into four patties.

2 Heat olive oil in a medium cast iron skillet over medium heat. Place 1-2 burger patties on skillet and cook 4 minutes on each side. Repeat with remaining burgers. Assemble burgers on buns and top with suggested toppings. Enjoy immediately.

GROUND BEEF ITALIAN MEATBALLS

PREP
15
MINUTES

COOK
45
MINUTES

TOTAL
60
MINUTES

SERVES
5

P CERTIFIED PALEO · CERTIFIED PALEO

K KETO FRIENDLY · KETO FRIENDLY

GLUTEN FREE · GLUTEN FREE

DAIRY FREE · DAIRY FREE

Enjoy the flavor of old world Italian meatballs in this Paleo version. Blanched almond flour steps in for breadcrumbs while herbs like fennel seed, basil and oregano season ground beef for Italian flavor in every bite. Best of all, they're ready to eat in 1 hour from start to finish.

INGREDIENTS:

- 1 lb. 80/20 ground beef
- 1 large egg
- 24 oz. Paleo friendly pasta sauce
- 1/2 cup blanched almond flour
- 1/3 cup finely chopped parsley
- 1 tsp. dried oregano
- 1 tsp. dried basil
- 1/2 tsp. garlic powder

- 1/2 tsp. fennel seed
- Pinch of nutmeg
- 1 Tbsp. olive oil
- 1 tsp. sea salt
- 1/4 cup fresh chopped basil for serving

EQUIPMENT:

- Medium skillet

DIRECTIONS:

1 Combine ground beef, almond flour, egg, parsley, fennel seed, oregano, basil, garlic, sea salt and nutmeg in a large mixing bowl. Using hands, mix thoroughly until evenly incorporated.

2 Form into 10 meatballs and place on a plate. Heat olive oil over medium-high heat in a medium skillet for 1 minute. Add 4-5 meatballs to hot skillet and brown for 4 minutes. Turn and brown an additional 4 minutes. Place browned meatballs on a plate while cooking the rest.

3 Add all meatballs to pan and pour in pasta sauce. Bring to a boil. Reduce heat to medium-low and simmer for 30 minutes or until center of meatballs are cooked through, turning meatballs after 15 minutes. Serve hot topped with fresh basil.

TERIYAKI BBQ MEATBALLS

PREP
5
MINUTES

COOK
42
MINUTES

TOTAL
47
MINUTES

SERVES
4

If you're in need of a crowd-pleasing recipe that is the perfect two-bite munchie, look no further than these teriyaki meatballs. Asian flavors simmer together in a tomato sauce for a barbecue style sauce that is sweet, nutty and lip-smacking good!

The sauce can be used on chicken or pork as a marinade or for basting while grilling. When it comes time to enjoy the meatballs, you can stick toothpicks in them on a serving platter for easy serving or spoon the meatballs and sauce over cauliflower rice, zucchini noodles or traditional white rice for non-Paleo. Store leftovers in an airtight container in the refrigerator for up to 1 week.

INGREDIENTS:

- 1 lb. 80/20 ground beef
- 1 cup blanched almond flour
- 1 large pasture-raised egg
- 1 tsp. minced garlic
- 1 tsp. grated ginger
- 1 tsp. chili flakes
- 1/2 tsp. sea salt
- 2 Tbsp. avocado oil for cooking
- 1/4 cup green onion, finely chopped + extra for serving
- 1 tsp. sesame seeds for garnish

For Teriyaki BBQ Sauce:

- 1 cup unsweetened tomato sauce
- 1/2 cup coconut aminos
- 2 Tbsp. toasted sesame oil
- 2 Tbsp. raw honey
- 1/2 tsp. chili powder
- 1/4 tsp. garlic powder

EQUIPMENT:

- Small mixing bowl
- Medium mixing bowl
- Medium sauté pan
- Tongs
- Parchment paper

DIRECTIONS:

1 In a small mixing bowl, stir together ingredients for teriyaki barbecue sauce until smooth. Set aside.

2 In a separate medium sized mixing bowl, combine all ingredients for meatballs except green onions, sesame seeds and avocado oil. Mix thoroughly to combine.

3 Form meat mixture into approximately 18 meatballs and place on a large piece of parchment paper. Heat 2 tablespoons of avocado oil over medium heat in a medium sauté pan. Working in 2 batches, add meatballs and brown for 6 minutes, rolling meatballs around in pan every 1-2 minutes for even browning. Remove first batch of meatballs from skillet and set aside on a plate. Repeat with second batch.

4 Reduce heat to low and add all meatballs to pan. Pour teriyaki barbecue sauce over meatballs. Simmer meatballs for 30 minutes or until completely cooked through, stirring occasionally. Serve hot, garnished with sesame seeds and green onion.

TACO STUFFED SWEET POTATOES

PREP
10
MINUTES

COOK
75
MINUTES

TOTAL
85
MINUTES

SERVES
4

Enjoy all the flavor of a zesty taco without sacrificing flavor! Ground beef is seasoned with warm spices in a tangy tomato sauce before filling into sweet potatoes for a drool-worthy Paleo dinner that is perfectly portioned.

TIP! When choosing sweet potatoes, look for medium sized spuds with a uniform shape, this will help them bake evenly and lay flat when sliced and filled.

INGREDIENTS:

- 1 lb. ground beef
- 4 medium sweet potatoes
- 1 tsp. avocado oil
- 1/2 cup tomato sauce
- 1 Tbsp. ground cumin
- 1 tsp. smoked paprika
- 1 tsp. dried oregano
- 1/4 tsp. cayenne pepper
- 1/4 tsp. onion powder
- 1/2 tsp. sea salt

For Avocado Salsa Fresca:

- 1 medium ripe avocado, diced
- 1 cup chopped tomato
- 1/2 cup chopped red onion
- 1/3 cup chopped cilantro
- Juice of half a lime
- 1 tsp. minced jalapeño
- 1/4 tsp. sea salt

EQUIPMENT:

- Medium baking pan
- Medium cast iron skillet
- Small mixing bowl

DIRECTIONS:

1 Preheat oven to 375°F and grease potato skins with avocado oil. Place sweet potatoes on a baking sheet lined with parchment paper. Bake for 1 hour. Cool sweet potatoes at room temperature while preparing other ingredients.

2 Heat ground beef in a medium skillet over medium heat. Use a spatula to breakup beef into crumbles. Cook 10 minutes, stirring occasionally. Stir in dry seasonings and tomato sauce until thoroughly combined. Simmer for 5 minutes.

3 While taco meat cooks, combine ingredients for avocado salsa in a small bowl. Stir well. Set aside.

4 Slice sweet potatoes down center lengthwise and fill with taco meat mixture. Top with avocado salsa. Serve right away.

GARLIC BUTTER RIBEYE STEAK BITES

PREP
5
MINUTES

COOK
10
MINUTES

TOTAL
15
MINUTES

SERVES
4

These garlic butter steak bites are a meat lovers delight! They can be enjoyed as a high-protein snack to curb hunger or served alongside sauteed vegetables for a complete meal. The garlicky steak bites are ready to eat in just 15 minutes and cleanup is a breeze!

INGREDIENTS:

- 1 lb. ribeye steak, cut into bite sized cubes
- 4 Tbsp. unsalted grass fed butter
- 2 tsp. minced garlic
- 1 tsp. sea salt
- 1/4 tsp. cracked black pepper
- 1 Tbsp. chopped parsley

EQUIPMENT:

- Large skillet

DIRECTIONS:

1 Season cubed steak with 1 teaspoon of sea salt on all sides.

2 Melt butter in a large skillet over medium high-heat. Add the steak and sear until browned, flipping halfway through, 6 to 8 minutes total.

3 Add the garlic and pepper and cook for 1 minute more. Remove from heat and garnish with chopped parsley. Serve hot.

SHEET PAN RIBEYE FAJITAS

PREP
15
MINUTES

COOK
34
MINUTES

TOTAL
49
MINUTES

SERVES
4

This sheet pan meal is ready for the table in under an hour! High-protein ribeye steaks are roasted in smoky Mexican spices with bell pepper and onion for an easy meal with minimal prep work. Serve over Paleo-compliant tortillas if desired.

INGREDIENTS:

- 2 boneless ribeye steaks
- 1 Tbsp. olive oil
- 2 Tbsp. coconut aminos
- 1 Tbsp. lime juice
- 1 Tbsp. ground cumin
- 1 tsp. dried oregano
- 1/4 tsp. garlic powder
- 1/4 tsp. smoked paprika
- 1/8 tsp. cayenne pepper

For Vegetables:

- 2 medium bell peppers, thinly sliced
- 1 small sweet white onion, thinly sliced
- 1 Tbsp. olive oil

For Serving:

- 1 tsp. sea salt
- 1/4 tsp. cracked black pepper
- 1/4 cup chopped cilantro
- 1 lime, sliced into wedges

EQUIPMENT:

- Baking sheet

DIRECTIONS:

1 Preheat oven to 450°F and lightly grease a medium baking sheet with olive oil.

2 Stir together coconut aminos, lime juice, olive oil, cumin, oregano, garlic powder, smoked paprika and cayenne in a small bowl to form a thick marinade. Blot excess moisture off steaks with a paper towel and place into a shallow bowl. Pour marinade on steaks and coat both sides. Set aside to marinate for 10 minutes while preparing other ingredients.

3 Scatter bell peppers and onions slices on baking sheet and drizzle with olive oil. Toss to coat. Place steaks onto center of baking sheet and bake for 13-15 minutes.

4 Turn oven to broil and broil 3-4 minutes longer. Season steak and vegetables with sea salt and pepper. Rest steaks for 5 minutes before slicing against the grain into strips. Serve warm topped with cilantro and extra lime wedges.

ONE POT SHORT RIB BEEF STEW

PREP
10
MINUTES

COOK
5
HOURS

TOTAL
5+
HOURS

SERVES
4

This fall off the bone beef stew uses short ribs for big beef flavor in a savory stock with hearty vegetables. Beef is seared in ghee to add rich flavor to the cooking liquid and brown the beef, enhancing its flavor as well. Serve over mashed cauliflower for a complete meal.

INGREDIENTS:

- 3 1/2 to 4 lbs. beef short ribs
- 2 Tbsp. ghee
- 2 tsp. minced garlic
- 2 Tbsp. tomato paste
- 4 cups beef stock
- 2 sprigs fresh thyme
- 1 sprig fresh rosemary
- 2 cups peeled/chopped sweet potatoes

- 1 cup coarsely chopped carrot
- 1 cup coarsely chopped celery
- 1 cup chopped sweet white onion
- 1/2 tsp. sea salt
- 1/4 tsp. cracked black pepper

EQUIPMENT:

- Heavy pot or Dutch oven

DIRECTIONS:

1 Heat ghee in a heavy pot or Dutch oven over medium-high heat for 2 minutes. Blot short ribs dry with paper towel and add to pot.

2 Brown for 2-3 minutes on each side. Add garlic to pot and sauté 1 minute. Pour beef stock into pan and deglaze, scraping up any browned bits on the pan with a wooden spatula.

3 Add tomato paste, thyme and rosemary to pot and cover with lid. Reduce heat to medium low and simmer for 3 hours.

4 Add chopped onion, celery, sweet potatoes and carrots to pot and cover with lid slightly cracked. Cook an additional 2 hours or until meat easily falls off of bone. Season with salt and pepper and enjoy hot.

HATCH PORTOBELLO + SKIRT STEAK LETTUCE CUPS

PREP
15
MINUTES

COOK
15
MINUTES

TOTAL
65
MINUTES

SERVES
4

This Paleo twist on tacos uses Bibb lettuce as a light and refreshing cup for serving cumin-lime marinated skirt steak, hearty portobello mushrooms and a creamy avocado dressing. This is a high-protein recipe that feeds hungry appetites!

INGREDIENTS:

- 1 lb. grass fed skirt steak

  For Marinade:

- 1/4 cup lime juice
- 2 Tbsp. coconut aminos
- 2 Tbsp. avocado oil
- 1 tsp. ground cumin
- 1/2 tsp. sea salt
- 1/4 tsp. black pepper
- 1 tsp. minced garlic

  For Dressing:

- 1 ripe avocado
- 1/4 cup fresh lime juice
- 1/4 cup filtered water
- 2 Tbsp. fresh chopped cilantro
- 1/2 tsp. minced garlic
- 1/2 tsp. sea salt

For Filling:

- 1 Tbsp. avocado oil
- 1 cup sliced baby portobello mushrooms
- 4 oz. can hatch green chiles
- 1/2 cup cilantro
- 2 limes, sliced into wedges
- 8 Bibb lettuce leaves
- 2 Tbsp. shelled pumpkin seeds

EQUIPMENT:

- Blender
- Large skillet

DIRECTIONS:

1 Add ingredients for avocado dressing in a blender and blend for 10 seconds. Refrigerate until serving.

2 Combine ingredients for marinade in a shallow dish. Add steak and coat on both sides. Marinate at room temperature for 30 minutes.

3 Heat a large skillet over high heat. Add 1 tablespoon of oil and cook for 1 minute until very hot. Add steak and sear, approximately 4-5 minutes per side. Remove from heat and let rest at least 10 minutes before slicing.

4 While steak is resting, add hatch chiles to pan steak was cooked in. Cook over medium high heat for about 3 minutes. Add portobello mushrooms and cook until mushrooms and chiles have some char.

5 Make lettuce cups by adding steak topped with hatch chiles and portobellos. Top with cilantro and pumpkin seeds. Serve with lime wedges and avocado dressing.

BALSAMIC MUSHROOM STEAK BITES

PREP
15
MINUTES

COOK
12
MINUTES

TOTAL
27
MINUTES

SERVES
4

P CERTIFIED PALEO

K KETO FRIENDLY

GLUTEN FREE

These seared Balsamic steak bites pack a ton of flavor and are easy to throw together! To turn them into a complete meal, asparagus and tender mushrooms are added. The sauce is a tangy Balsamic ghee with plenty of fresh garlic that smothers the steak and veggies.

INGREDIENTS:

- 2 lbs. sirloin steak
- 1 bunch asparagus, sliced into 2 inch pieces
- 3 cups cremini mushrooms, halved
- 2 tsp, minced garlic
- 1 Tbsp. ghee
- 2 1/2 Tbsp. Balsamic vinegar (divided)
- 1 1/2 tsp. sea salt (divided)
- Black pepper to taste

EQUIPMENT:

- Large cast iron skillet

DIRECTIONS:

1 Remove steak from the fridge about 15 minutes before cooking so it can come to room temp and slice into bite size pieces. Season all over with 1 teaspoon of salt and pepper.

2 Heat ghee in a large cast iron skillet over medium-high high heat for 2 minutes.

3 Sear steak in the skillet for about 2-3 minutes, stirring once. Add 1 tablespoon of Balsamic vinegar to the pan, coat steak with Balsamic.

4 Add asparagus and mushrooms to the skillet and 1/2 teaspoon of salt and remaining vinegar. Cook veggies for about 5 minutes. Add minced garlic in the last 2 minutes. Transfer to serving bowls and enjoy hot.

BLACKBERRY SIRLOIN SALAD

PREP
10
MINUTES

COOK
10
MINUTES

TOTAL
45
MINUTES

SERVES
4

Savory and fruity flavors unite in this salad that serves as a main dish. Balsamic sirloin steak, cucumbers, blackberries and crunchy pistachios are served over a bed of mixed greens and drizzled in a fruity blackberry basil dressing. This salad is delicious year round but especially during peak blackberry season or on a warm summer day.

INGREDIENTS:

- 1 lb. sirloin steak
- 1 Tbsp. avocado oil
- 2 Tbsp. Balsamic vinegar
- Sea salt and black pepper to taste

For Salad:

- 3 cups mixed greens
- 1 cup microgreens
- 1/2 cup blackberries
- 1 Persian cucumber, sliced
- 1/2 cup thinly sliced red onion
- 1/4 cup chopped pistachios

For Dressing:

- 2 Tbsp. lemon juice
- 2 Tbsp. Balsamic vinegar
- 1 Tbsp. raw honey
- 1/2 cup blackberries
- 1/4 cup olive oil
- 1/4 cup fresh basil leaves
- Pinch of sea salt

EQUIPMENT:

- Grill
- Blender

DIRECTIONS:

1 Sprinkle salt and pepper on steak on all sides. Pat down into steak. Coat with avocado oil and Balsamic vinegar. Let rest at least 15 minutes.

2 Preheat outdoor or indoor grill to medium high heat. Place steak on grill. Cook 4-5 minutes per side, depending on thickness of steak and desired doneness. Remove from heat and let rest 10 minutes before slicing.

3 Make dressing by combining all ingredients together in a blender. Set in refrigerator until ready to use.

4 Top greens with blackberries, cucumbers, pistachios, microgreens and red onion. Serve with blackberry dressing.

BULGOGI BEEF BOWLS

PREP
10
MINUTES

COOK
10
MINUTES

MARINADE
2
HOURS

TOTAL
2.5
HOURS

SERVES
2

Bulgogi is a popular Korean recipe that means "fire meat." It can be grilled or cooked in a hot pan; using pork or beef. The recipe gets a kick of heat thanks to a bright red spice called gochugaru. Although it looks super spicy, the heat is actually quite balanced and less intense than cayenne.

This recipe is light enough for summer and hefty enough to enjoy during the winter making it perfect for your year round recipe arsenal!

TIP! Look for gochugaru in the Asian foods section of your local grocer or it can be purchased online.

INGREDIENTS:

- 1 lb. sirloin steak

  For Marinade:

- 1 Tbsp. gochugaru
- 1 Tbsp. coconut sugar
- 1 Tbsp. apple cider vinegar
- 2 Tbsp. coconut aminos
- 2 Tbsp. toasted sesame oil
- 1 clove garlic, minced
- 1 tsp. grated ginger
- 1/2 tsp. sea salt

For Bowl:

- 2 tsp. olive oil, divided
- 2 medium zucchini, spiral sliced on 3mm blade
- 2 Tbsp. jalapeño, thinly sliced
- 1 cup cucumber, thinly sliced
- 1/2 cup pickled red onion
- 1 Tbsp. sesame seeds

EQUIPMENT:

- Shallow dish with lid
- Medium pan
- Tongs

DIRECTIONS:

1 Stir together ingredients for marinade in a shallow dish to form a paste. Slice steak into thin pieces and place into marinade. Stir well to coat. Cover and refrigerate for 2 hours.

2 Heat 1 teaspoon of olive oil in a medium pan over medium heat. Add zucchini noodles and cook for 3-4 minutes tossing occasionally. Divide noodles among 4 bowls.

3 Wipe pan clean and return to stove over medium-high heat. Add remaining teaspoon of olive oil and heat for 2 minutes. Use tongs to transfer slices of steak to pan working in 2 batches. Sear steak for 1 minute on each side. Remove steak from pan and set aside. Repeat with remaining steak.

4 Divide steak among bowls and top with jalapeños, cucumber, pickled red onion and sesame seeds. Serve immediately.

SESAME GINGER SHEET PAN STEAK AND VEGETABLES

PREP
10
MINUTES

COOK
25
MINUTES

TOTAL
35
MINUTES

SERVES
4

This quick and easy Asian-inspired meal is a one pan wonder! Unlike many takeout options, there's no soy or preservatives added. This gives you control over the quality of ingredients for a protein-rich meal with the goodness of grass fed beef. The sauce is made using coconut aminos instead of soy sauce for a rich flavor without any gluten or soy. Nutty toasted sesame oil adds aroma and flavor to the dish while fresh ginger and garlic pack anti-inflammatory compounds. This sauce also doubles as a marinade for steak or chicken.

INGREDIENTS:

- 2 lbs. sirloin steak, cubed
- 1 red bell pepper, diced
- 1/2 a medium red onion, coarsely chopped
- 2 cups shishito peppers
- 2 cups broccoli florets
- 1/2 cup cilantro, chopped
- 1 tsp. sesame seeds

  For Sauce:

- 1/2 cup coconut aminos
- 2 Tbsp. toasted sesame oil
- 2 Tbsp. apple cider vinegar
- 1 tsp. coconut sugar
- 1/2 tsp. minced garlic
- 1/2 tsp. minced ginger
- 1 tsp. tapioca starch

EQUIPMENT:

- Saucepan
- Whisk
- Sheet pan
- Parchment paper

DIRECTIONS:

1 Preheat oven to 400°F and line a 15x10 baking sheet with parchment paper. Combine all ingredients for sauce except tapioca starch in a small saucepan over low heat. When mixture starts to bubble, gradually whisk in tapioca starch. Continue to heat for 2 minutes or until thickened. Remove from heat and set aside to cool for 10 minutes.

2 Place cubed steak onto baking sheet and drizzle with 2 tablespoons of the sauce. Bake for 8 minutes.

3 Scatter vegetables onto baking sheet and drizzle with 3 tablespoons of sauce. Bake for 12 minutes. Broil for 3 minutes or until veggies and steak are lightly browned on top. Remove from oven and drizzle with remaining sauce, chopped cilantro and sesame seeds. Serve hot.

STRIP STEAK WITH CHIVE + PARSLEY GREMOLATA

PREP
10
MINUTES

COOK
10
MINUTES

TOTAL
25
MINUTES

SERVES
2

For a healthy meal that doesn't skimp on flavor try these seared strip steaks topped with a tangy herb gremolata. It's a high protein meal that will fill you up without weighing you down. Gremolata is a fresh herb topping, full of garlic, lemon and fresh green herbs like parsley, cilantro or basil. Serve steaks over a mixed green salad, cauliflower rice, or roasted vegetables.

INGREDIENTS:

- 2 -6 oz. strip steaks
- 2 Tbsp. avocado oil
- 1/2 tsp. sea salt
- 1/4 tsp. cracked black pepper

For Gremolata:

- 1/4 cup avocado oil
- 1 cup fresh curly parsley
- 2 Tbsp. fresh chopped chives
- 2 Tbsp. lemon juice

- 1 Tbsp. lemon zest
- 2 cloves garlic
- 1/4 tsp. sea salt
- Salad greens

EQUIPMENT:

- Food processor
- Skillet
- Small serving bowl

DIRECTIONS:

1 Combine ingredients for gremolata in a food processor and blend until thoroughly combined. Transfer to a small serving bowl and set aside.

2 Heat a large skillet over medium high heat. Drizzle steaks with avocado oil and season with salt and pepper on both sides. Place steaks on hot pan and sear for 3-4 minutes on each side. Transfer to a cutting board to rest for 5 minutes.

3 Slice steaks thinly against the grain and serve over a bed of salad greens topped with gremolata.

HERB ROASTED TRI-TIP WITH RUTABAGA

PREP
10
MINUTES

COOK
60
MINUTES

MARINADE
4-8
HOURS

TOTAL
70
MINUTES

SERVES
2-3

This melt in your mouth herb tri-tip roast is the perfect meal for elegant dinner parties or holidays. It roasts in a fraction of the time, unlike tougher cuts of beef, due to its tender texture. Serve alongside roasted root veggies and horseradish for a mouthwatering meal that doesn't require a lot of fuss!

INGREDIENTS:

- 2 lb. tri-tip beef
- 2 Tbsp. ghee
- 2 Tbsp. olive oil
- 2 Tbsp. coconut aminos
- 2 Tbsp. fresh thyme leaves, chopped
- 2 cloves garlic, minced
- 1/2 tsp. dried rosemary
- 1 tsp. sea salt
- 1/2 tsp. cracked black pepper

For Roasted Rutabaga:

- 2 lbs. rutabaga, peeled/ coarsely chopped
- 1/2 tsp. dried rosemary
- 1 tsp. minced garlic
- 1/4 tsp. sea salt
- Olive oil

EQUIPMENT:

- Roasting pan
- Cast iron skillet
- Small bowl
- Parchment paper
- Cooling rack

DIRECTIONS:

1 Combine olive oil, coconut aminos, thyme, rosemary, garlic, sea salt and black pepper in a small bowl. Place tri-tip in a shallow bowl and cover with marinade. Use hands to rub marinade on the top side of meat. Cover and refrigerate 4-8 hours.

2 Preheat oven to 400ºF and line a roasting pan with parchment paper and place a cooling rack on top.

3 Remove beef from marinade and blot with paper towel to remove excess surface moisture. Heat ghee a large cast iron skillet over medium-high heat for 2 minutes. Sear beef on pan for 4 minutes on each side.

4 Transfer to roasting pan on rack with fat cap facing down and roast for 20-30 minutes until internal temperature reaches 135ºF for rare and 145ºF for medium rare. Rest tri-tip on a cutting board for 15 minutes before slicing.

5 While steak rests, increase oven temperature to 425ºF. Combine rutabaga, olive oil, rosemary, sea salt and garlic in a medium mixing bowl. Spread on a parchment paper lined baking sheet and bake for 15-20 minutes. Slice tri-tip and serve with roasted rutabaga.

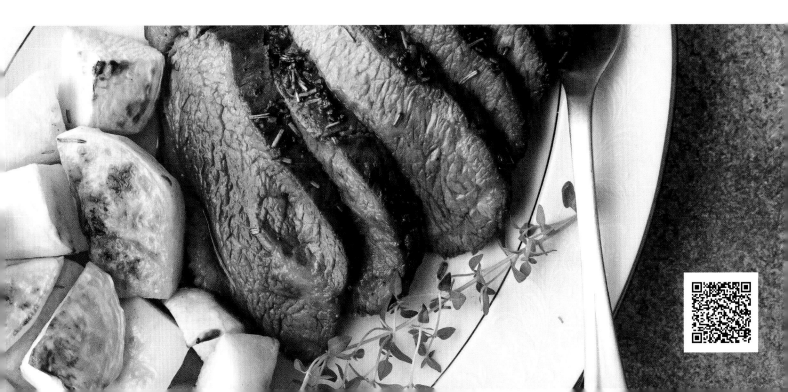

PASTURE-RAISED PORK

MORE THAN JUST ORGANIC

Wild Pastures' pigs spend their lives on pasture, foraging and exercising as they please. Most commercial pigs are kept in confinement crates and never see pasture. "Organic pork" can also be deceiving since there is no requirement for the pigs to ever step foot on a pasture. Thanks to their ability to forage freely, pasture-raised pigs are healthier and have much higher levels of nutrients.

Our pigs are fed a pasture-based, non-GMO diet consisting mostly of grass on pesticide-free pastures and non-GMO foods such as turnips, apples, pumpkins, etc.

They are raised in the USA by small, family farmers without antibiotics, steroids, or hormones.

BACON-WRAPPED SWEET POTATO BITES

PREP
10
MINUTES

COOK
40
MINUTES

TOTAL
50
MINUTES

SERVES
3-4

These bacon-wrapped sweet potato bites make a great, healthy appetizer for a football watch-party or a delicious side with dinner. The sweetness of the coconut oil and maple syrup combined with the salty bacon form a flavor bomb in your mouth!

INGREDIENTS:

- 10 slices sugar-free bacon
- 1 lb sweet potatoes
- 2 Tbsp. coconut oil
- 2 tsp. maple syrup
- 1/4 tsp. paprika
- 1/4 tsp. black pepper
- 1/4 tsp. sea salt

EQUIPMENT:

- Baking sheet
- Mixing bowl
- Toothpicks

DIRECTIONS:

1 Preheat oven to 400ºF and line baking sheet with parchment paper.

2 Cut the sweet potatoes into thick rounds (1" should be thick enough for the bacon to wrap around). Mix with coconut oil, maple syrup and and seasonings in a bowl.

3 Wrap half slices of bacon around the edges of the sweet potato rounds overlapping slightly. Secure with toothpicks and place onto the baking sheet.

4 Bake for 35-40 minutes,. Move bites onto a paper towel to catch excess oil. Serve.

BACON ZUCCHINI FRITTERS

PREP
20
MINUTES

COOK
5-10
MINUTES

TOTAL
30
MINUTES

PORTIONS
14-16

If you're craving hash browns or french fries but don't want to ruin your diet, these bacon-zucchini fritters are for you. They're unbelievably easy to make, low calorie, and the perfect way to sneak some veggies into your meal without feeling like you're eating veggies! Parents of picky kids: this ones for you!

INGREDIENTS:

- 6 slices sugar-free bacon, crumbled
- 4 cups grated/shredded zucchini about 2-3 medium
- 3/4 tsp. salt to "sweat" the zucchini
- 2 Tbsp. coconut flour
- 2 Tbsp. arrowroot flour
- 1 large egg whisked
- 1/2 tsp. onion powder
- 1/4 tsp. garlic powder
- 1/4-1/2 tsp. black pepper
- 2-3 Tbsp. coconut oil

EQUIPMENT:

- Grater
- Sauté skillet
- Colander
- Large bowl
- Wide spatula
- Wire cooling rack

DIRECTIONS:

1 Begin by "sweating" the grated zucchini (this draws out the excess moisture so your fritters aren't soggy!). Place in a colander over a bowl and add a dash of salt. Let sit for 15-20 minutes. Remove from colander and pat/squeeze out any excess moisture with a paper towel.

2 While the zucchini is drying out, cook the bacon until crispy. Remove from pan, let cool for a few minutes, then crumble.

3 In a large bowl, combine the zucchini, crumbled bacon, coconut flour, arrowroot, egg, onion powder, garlic powder, and pepper.

4 Heat a large skillet over medium heat, adding 1 tablespoon coconut oil. Scoop the fritters mixture in heaping tablespoons into the skillet and gently press down to about 1/2" thickness. Keeping the size of the fritters smaller makes them easier to flip and remove from the pan.

5 After 2-3 minutes, carefully flip using a wide spatula. Fry on the second side another 2-3 minutes until golden brown, lowering the heat a bit if necessary. Carefully remove to a wire rack while you make the rest.

6 Add additional oil for each batch, and don't be afraid to adjust the temperature to keep them from burning.

7 Serve hot with a Paleo mayo or a spicy dipping sauce of your choice.

BLTA SLAW

PREP
6
MINUTES

COOK
15
MINUTES

TOTAL
30
MINUTES

PORTIONS
4

This versatile slaw works great as a side at your next cookout or is delicious on its own for a refreshing, summer lunch. The apple cider vinegar adds a tangy flavor with a ton of health benefits like supporting healthy blood sugar, decreasing bloating, and more! This is a meal you can feel good about.

INGREDIENTS:

- 6-8 strips sugar-free bacon
- 1 head Napa cabbage, shredded
- 1 Tbsp. olive oil
- 1 lime, juiced
- 1 1/2 Tbsp. apple cider vinegar
- 1/4 tsp. red pepper flakes
- 1/2 tsp. garlic powder
- 1/2 tsp. onion powder
- 1/2 tsp. salt
- 1/2 tsp. pepper
- 1/2 cup shredded carrots

- 1 pint grape tomatoes, cut in half
- 1/4 cup chives, chopped
- 1/4 cup parsley, chopped
- 1/4 cup cilantro
- 1 avocado, chopped

EQUIPMENT:

- Baking sheet
- Parchment paper
- Large bowl

DIRECTIONS:

1 Preheat oven to 375°F. Lay bacon out on a parchment lined baking sheet. Bake until crispy, approximately 15 minutes. Keep bacon fat. Slice bacon into strips once cooled.

2 In a large bowl, combine cabbage, olive oil, lime juice, apple cider vinegar, red pepper flakes, garlic powder, onion powder, salt and pepper. Mix well and let rest at least 15 minutes to tenderize cabbage.

3 Add grape tomatoes, carrots, chives, parsley and cilantro to cabbage. Toss to combine.

4 Just before serving, top slaw with bacon and avocado.

CARAMELIZED ONION + BACON SOUP

PREP
5
MINUTES

COOK
50
MINUTES

TOTAL
60
MINUTES

SERVES
2

This alternative version of a French onion soup includes bacon for a heartier rendition of a classic dish. For the traditional French onion look, add cheese to the top and broil. This dish is the perfect meal to warm up on a cold wintery evening.

INGREDIENTS:

- 6 slices of sugar-free bacon, cut into 1-inch pieces

- 3 large yellow onions, halved and thinly sliced lengthwise

- 4 cups low-sodium beef broth

Optional toppings: cheese

EQUIPMENT:

- Dutch oven or stock pot

DIRECTIONS:

1 In a medium dutch oven or stock pot over medium-high heat, cook bacon stirring occasionally, until browned.

2 Pour off all but 1 tablespoon of bacon fat from the pot. Add the onions and reduce heat to medium-low.

3 Stirring occasionally and scraping up browned bits from the pot with a wooden spoon, cook until onions are very soft and deep golden brown. This process takes about 45-60 minutes. Once the onions are very soft and caramelized, add the beef broth and bring to a boil.

4 Remove from heat and serve immediately.

SHAVED BRUSSELS SPROUT, BACON + PEAR SALAD

PREP
6-8
MINUTES

COOK
40
MINUTES

TOTAL
48
MINUTES

SERVES
4-6

This is one of the best salads for spring and summer when pears are in season. When paired with pasture-raised bacon, the salty sweet combo makes a drool-worthy meal. Serve at your next cookout with grass fed beef burgers or enjoy on its own for a healthy, filling lunch.

INGREDIENTS:

- 6-8 strips sugar-free bacon
- 2 lbs. Brussels sprouts, shaved
- 2 pears, seeds removed and chopped
- 1/4 red onion, very thinly sliced
- 4 Tbsp. pecan pieces, toasted

  For Vinaigrette:
- 2 garlic cloves
- 3 Tbsp. apple cider vinegar
- 3 Tbsp. bacon fat
- 4 Tbsp. water
- Pinch of sea salt and pepper

EQUIPMENT:

- Large bowl
- Baking sheet
- Blender
- Parchment paper

DIRECTIONS:

1 Preheat oven to 375°F. Lay bacon out on a parchment lined baking sheet. Bake until crispy, approximately 15-20 minutes. Remove bacon from tray, reserving bacon fat, and place on paper towels to absorb fat. Slice into matchsticks once cooled.

2 Increase oven temperature to 400°F. Toss shaved Brussels sprouts with 1 tablespoon of bacon fat and sprinkle with salt and pepper. Roast for 15-20 minutes or until leaves are browned and crispy.

3 Make bacon vinaigrette. In a blender mix ingredients together until smooth. Set aside until ready to use.

4 Toss Brussels sprouts with bacon vinaigrette. Top with bacon matchsticks, pears, red onion and pecan pieces.

SWEET POTATO + BACON STEW

PREP
5
MINUTES

COOK
50
MINUTES

TOTAL
55
MINUTES

SERVES
6-8

If you want a hearty, warming, filling stew perfect for the winter months - this is it. Sweet potatoes and bacon make up the heart of this stew. Their flavors are brought out even more by the addition of peppers, onions, and orange zest that is like a flavor bomb in your mouth.

INGREDIENTS:

- 4 slices sugar-free bacon, diced
- 1 medium orange, zest and juice
- 2 lbs. (6 med) sweet potatoes, diced small
- 6 cups chicken broth
- 2 large onions, diced
- 2 red bell peppers, diced
- 4 garlic cloves, minced
- 1 cup loosely packed fresh cilantro leaves, finely chopped

- 1 tsp. dried Italian seasoning
- 1 Tbsp. ground cumin
- 1 Tbsp. chipotle chili powder
- 1 tsp. red pepper flakes
- 1/2 tsp. salt

EQUIPMENT:

- Large stock pot

DIRECTIONS:

1 In a large stock pot over medium-high heat, cook the bacon pieces until browned and the fat is rendered.

2 Add the onions, peppers, garlic, orange zest and red pepper flakes and sauté until onions begin to turn translucent.

3 Add the sweet potatoes, broth, and spices and bring to a boil. Lower the heat to a simmer, cover and cook until potatoes are cooked through and fork tender (but not mushy), roughly 40-50 minutes.

4 When the soup is cooked, add the juice from the orange and the cilantro and stir to combine.

DIJON PORK CHOPS WITH PARSNIPS + THYME MASH

PREP
5
MINUTES

COOK
20
MINUTES

TOTAL
25
MINUTES

SERVES
2

Also known as a Boston butt or pork blade, pork steaks are cut from the shoulder of the pig and are known for having lean, tender meat. With this recipe the pork is coated in almond meal to add a delicious crunch to an otherwise tender cut of pork. Omit ghee to make this recipe dairy-free and Paleo friendly.

INGREDIENTS:

- 4 boneless pork chops
- 1/3 cup Dijon mustard + 1/4 cup set aside
- 1 1/2 Tbsp. fresh chopped thyme
- 1 Tbsp. nutritional yeast
- 1 tsp. dried dill
- 1/4 tsp. sea salt
- 2 Tbsp. avocado oil or ghee
- 1 lb parsnips, peeled and diced

- 2 Tbsp. olive oil + 1 Tbsp. separated
- 2 Tbsp. coconut milk (unsweetened, full-fat)
- 3 tsp. dried thyme

EQUIPMENT:

- Large skillet
- Large pot
- Food processor

DIRECTIONS:

1 Heat ghee or avocado oil in a large skillet over medium heat. Brush pork chops on all sides with Dijon, then place chops into the skillet and cook 8 minutes. Flip and cook for an additional 8 minutes.

2 While the chops are cooking, bring a large pot of water to a boil. Add the diced parsnips and boil for 15 to 20 minutes, until very tender. Drain, reserving 1/4 cup cooking water.

3 Place the parsnips in a food processor and puree until smooth. Add the olive oil and dried thyme; puree again until smooth, adding the coconut milk and a bit of reserved water, if needed, until very creamy.

4 In another small bowl, stir together 1/4 cup of Dijon mustard, olive oil, nutritional yeast, thyme, dill and sea salt.

5 Remove the pork chops from the skillet and serve with Dijon drizzled on top alongside mashed parsnips garnish with fresh thyme.

HOISIN GLAZED PORK CHOPS

PREP
5
MINUTES

COOK
65
MINUTES

TOTAL
70
MINUTES

SERVES
3-4

P CERTIFIED PALEO · CERTIFIED PALEO

K KETO FRIENDLY · KETO FRIENDLY

GLUTEN FREE · GLUTEN FREE

DAIRY FREE · DAIRY FREE

Cook up some pork chops with an Asian twist with this hoisin sesame glaze. Enjoy notes of nutty sesame, sweet coconut, and tangy ginger alongside asparagus for a delicious, well-rounded meal.

INGREDIENTS:

- 3-4 boneless pork chops
- 1 Tbsp. coconut oil
- 1-2 bunches asparagus
- 2 tsp. sesame oil
- 1/4 tsp. red pepper flakes
- 1/2 tsp. salt
- 1/2 tsp. pepper

For Hoisin Sauce:

- 1 Tbsp. coconut oil
- 3 garlic cloves, minced fine
- 1-inch piece ginger, minced fine

- 1/3 cup coconut aminos
- 2 Tbsp. tahini
- Zest and juice of 1 orange
- 1 Tbsp. apple cider vinegar
- 1 tsp. Chinese five spice
- 1/2 tsp. red pepper flakes
- Pinch salt and pepper

EQUIPMENT:

- Large skillet
- Medium saucepan

DIRECTIONS:

1 Sprinkle salt and pepper onto all sides of pork chops.

2 Make hoisin sauce. Heat a medium saucepan to medium heat. Add coconut oil and after another minute the garlic and ginger. Sauté for a couple minutes until the garlic and ginger are soft before adding the remaining ingredients. Simmer until sauce thickens, whisking for about 10 minutes. Remove from the heat and let cool.

3 Preheat oven to 375°F. Pour half of the hoisin sauce over the pork chops. Save remaining hoisin sauce for serving. Marinade pork chops for at least 30 minutes.

4 Toss asparagus with sesame oil, red pepper flakes, and a pinch of salt and pepper. Lay on a sheet tray. Bake al dente, 5-7 minutes.

5 Heat a large skillet over medium high heat. Add coconut oil and let heat for a minute. Sear pork chops on all sides, approximately 15 minutes total depending on thickness of chops. Let rest at least 10 minutes.

6 Serve pork chops and sesame asparagus with reserved hoisin sauce.

MANGO HABANERO PORK CHOPS WITH THYME GREEN BEANS

PREP
10
MINUTES

COOK
3-4
HOURS

TOTAL
3-4
HOURS

SERVES
3-4

Take your pork chops up a notch with this spicy, tangy mango habanero sauce. Paired with thyme green beans, this meal is full of fruits, vegetables, and a little flair. But the best part? You can cook it in a slow cooker, so it's a no-fuss way to have dinner on the table in seconds.

INGREDIENTS:

- 3-4 boneless pork chops
- 3/4 cup diced mango
- 1 small habanero, minced fine
- 1/4 lemon, juiced
- 2 garlic cloves, minced (divided)
- 3 Tbsp. ghee
- 4 cups green beans, trimmed

- 6 sprigs fresh thyme
- Salt and pepper
- Fresh thyme, for garnish

EQUIPMENT:

- Slow cooker
- Skillets (2)

DIRECTIONS:

1 Heat 1 tablespoon ghee in a skillet. Add diced mango and sauté until soft, about 5-6 minutes. Mash slightly, but leave a few chunks.

2 Transfer mango to a bowl and toss with habanero, lemon juice, garlic, and a pinch of salt and pepper.

3 Add pork chops to a slow cooker. Sprinkle with salt and pepper on all sides. Top with mango habanero sauce and toss to coat pork chops with sauce. Cook on high for 3-4 hours or low for 6 hours.

4 Once nearly cooked, heat another large skillet over medium-high heat. Add ghee and let heat for about 30 seconds. Add green beans, thyme, garlic, and a sprinkle of salt and pepper. Toss to combine.

5 Cook until green beans have browned bits and are al dente, stirring occasionally to cook evenly. Top green beans with mango habanero pork chops.

PORK WITH STONE FRUIT SALSA

PREP
7
MINUTES

COOK
10
MINUTES

TOTAL
17
MINUTES

SERVES
3-4

This quick and easy meal is one of the best things to do with your Wild Pastures' pork especially in the warmer months. With only 17 minutes total prep and cooking time, you'll have dinner on the table in no time. Feel free to double (or triple) the salsa recipe and serve it on the side with your favorite tortilla chips or dipping vegetables.

INGREDIENTS:

- 3-4 boneless or bone-in pork chops
- 1 peach
- 2 plums
- 1 tsp. lemon juice
- 1/4 cup thyme leaves, plus extra for garnish
- 1 tsp. avocado oil
- 1/2 tsp. garlic powder
- 1/4 tsp. ginger
- 1-2 shakes of cinnamon
- 1 tsp. salt

EQUIPMENT:

- Oven-safe skillet

DIRECTIONS:

1 Pat the pork dry and generously salt all over. Heat an oven safe skillet to high. Preheat oven to 400°F.

2 Combine the garlic powder, cinnamon and ginger together and season the pork Add more if you're using pork chops instead of tenderloin. Sear the pork in the hot skillet with avocado oil for 2 minutes, turn over, then put the skillet in the oven. Cook for about 8 minutes and check for doneness.

3 While the pork is cooking, make the salsa; chop the peach and plums, shred the thyme, and toss with lemon juice.

4 Serve pork topped with salsa and extra thyme leaves for garnish.

IRISH BEET + RED CABBAGE BRATWURST SKILLET

PREP
10
MINUTES

COOK
35
MINUTES

TOTAL
45
MINUTES

SERVES
2-4

Make this instead of your traditional corn beef and cabbage next St. Patrick's Day or enjoy as a creative weeknight meal! This Irish-inspired recipe using Wild Pastures bratwurst sausage is one of the most traditional ways possible for a filling, healthy meal that the whole family will love!

INGREDIENTS:

- 4 bratwurst sausage
- 3 cups of shredded red cabbage
- 1 cup grated beet
- 2 cloves of garlic, minced
- 1 Tbsp. bacon fat or lard (coconut oil can substitute)
- 1 Tbsp. apple cider vinegar
- 1 tsp. sea salt, divided
- Cracked black pepper, to taste

EQUIPMENT:

- Oven-safe skillet
- Grater

EQUIPMENT:

1 Preheat oven to 425°F. Place shredded cabbage, grated beet, and garlic in an oven-proof skillet, and combine with 1 tablespoon fat or oil, 1/2 teaspoon sea salt, and apple cider vinegar. Sprinkle with cracked black pepper.

2 Nestle the sausage between the beet and cabbage.

3 Bake for 20 minutes, then flip sausages and bake for 15 additional minutes. Serve with another dash of sea salt.

SLOW COOKER BRATWURST WITH APPLE-DIJON SAUERKRAUT

PREP
10
MINUTES

COOK
2-3
HOURS

TOTAL
3
HOURS

SERVES
6

This quick and easy recipe takes only 10 minutes of prep time making it the perfect weekday dinner when you feel like you don't have time to cook. Throw these in the crockpot at least 3 hours before you plan to eat for a great game day meal, Oktoberfest celebration, or just a cozy fall night in!

INGREDIENTS:

- 16 ounces bratwurst sausage, cut into 1-inch pieces
- 4 cups sauerkraut
- 1/2 yellow onion, sliced
- 1 Tbsp. olive or coconut oil
- 1 apple, diced
- 2 Tbsp. Dijon mustard
- 2 Tbsp. dill seed

EQUIPMENT:

- Slow cooker
- Saute pan

DIRECTIONS:

1 Heat olive or coconut oil over medium heat. Add onions and apples and sauté until fragrant, about 5-6 minutes.

2 Add all of the ingredients to a slow cooker and mix well. Cook on high for 2-3 hours or low for 4-6. Serve.

HERBED SAUSAGE GRAVY

PREP
10
MINUTES

COOK
20
MINUTES

TOTAL
30
MINUTES

SERVES
2-3

Wake up to this delicious, hearty breakfast of sausage and gravy. Similar to the classic British or Irish breakfast bangers and mash, this recipe has a few Wild Pastures changes. Made with sweet potatoes, this base perfectly absorbs the gravy. Taking only 20 - 30 minutes to make, you can get on with your day with a full stomach in no time.

INGREDIENTS:

- 1 lb. breakfast sausage
- 1 tsp. dried sage
- 1 tsp. fennel seed
- 3 Tbsp. olive oil
- 1 Tbsp. almond flour
- 2-3 Tbsp. tapioca flour
- 2 1/2-3 cups almond milk
- 4 medium sweet potatoes, diced and pan fried

EQUIPMENT:

- Skillet
- Whisk

DIRECTIONS:

1 In a large skillet, brown the sausage over medium heat, adding the sage and fennel. Once cooked, transfer it to a plate or bowl.

2 Add olive oil to the pan then stir in the almond and tapioca flour and combine well over medium heat.

3 Stir in the almond milk slowly and cook until the sauce has thickened. You may want to use a whisk for more thorough blending.

4 Add the sausage back in once thickened, then serve immediately over potatoes.

HERBED SAUSAGE GRAVY

BREAKFAST SAUSAGE QUICHE

PREP
10
MINUTES

COOK
73
MINUTES

TOTAL
83
MINUTES

SERVES
6-8

Hearty pasture-raised breakfast sausage combines in this high protein quiche with a buttery almond flour crust and plenty of vegetables. It's a meal that feeds a crowd! Pre-seasoned breakfast sausage is often full of sodium, added colors and preservatives, but this sausage is a step above using the goodness of pastured pork and natural seasoning.

Make meal prep easy! This quiche makes 6-8 servings and is ideal for a meal to have on hand during the busy week. Simply slice into servings and refrigerate. Reheat as needed.

INGREDIENTS:

- 1 lb. ground breakfast sausage
- 8 large eggs
- 1/4 cup unsweetened almond milk
- 1/2 cup chopped bell pepper
- 2 cups fresh spinach

  For Crust:

- 2 1/2 cups blanched almond flour
- 1 large egg at room temperature

- 1/3 cup melted butter + 1 tsp. for greasing
- 1/4 tsp. sea salt

EQUIPMENT:

- 9 inch round pie pan
- Medium cast iron pan
- Medium mixing bowl

WWW.WILDPASTURES.COM

DIRECTIONS:

1 Grease a 9-inch pie pan with 1 teaspoon melted butter. In a medium mixing bowl combine ingredients for crust and stir well to form a moist dough. Pour dough into pan and press with fingers to conform to pan.

2 Preheat oven to 350°F. Heat a medium cast iron pan over medium heat and add sausage. Use a wooden spatula to break up sausage into small pieces. Cook for 8 minutes. Drain grease from pan and return to stove. Stir in bell pepper and spinach. Cook an additional 5 minutes to wilt spinach. Remove from heat and transfer to a medium bowl to cool for 5 minutes.

3 Whisk together eggs and almond milk in a medium mixing bowl. Pour sausage mixture into eggs and stir. Pour into pie crust and bake for 55-60 minutes or until center is set. Remove from oven and cool for 10 minutes before slicing.

SPICY CAJUN BREAKFAST SKILLET

PREP
5 MINUTES

COOK
15 MINUTES

TOTAL
20 MINUTES

SERVES
4

Make room at the breakfast table! This spicy Cajun breakfast skillet is quick to make, fast to cleanup, and sure to please everyone. Loaded with spicy, Cajun flavors contrasted with sweet potatoes, this one will have people going back for seconds!

INGREDIENTS:

- 1 lb breakfast sausage
- 4 Tbsp. avocado oil or tallow (divided)
- 3 medium sweet potatoes, diced
- 2 tsp. Cajun or blackened seasoning
- 1 garlic clove, minced
- 1/2 medium yellow onion, diced
- 4 eggs
- Handful of spinach (optional)
- Chili flakes for garnish

EQUIPMENT:

- Stovetop skillet (2)

CARAMELIZED ONION + BACON SOUP

DIRECTIONS:

1 Heat 2 tablespoons oil in a skillet over medium heat. Add the potatoes, onion, garlic, and Cajun seasoning and cook until potatoes start to turn brown at the edges and the onions are caramelized.

2 Add in the sausage and continue cooking over medium heat until potatoes are tender and the sausage is cooked through. Stir occasionally. Once nearly finished, stir in a handful of spinach.

3 Heat the remaining oil over medium heat in a separate skillet while sausage and potatoes are cooking. Cook the eggs over easy, roughly one minute on each side.

4 Spoon sausage and potatoes onto plates and top with over easy eggs and chili flakes as a garnish.

MAPLE DIJON PORK CHOPS + CARROTS

PREP
5
MINUTES

COOK
30
MINUTES

TOTAL
35
MINUTES

SERVES
2

This one-pan recipe is the definition of wholesome Paleo cooking. With the comforting flavors of sweet maple syrup and woodsy rosemary, it's the perfect autumn dish. Best of all, it cooks up in 30 minutes flat!

Bone-in pork chops and tender petite carrots are complemented by the glossy sweet and savory sauce that smothers them. Rosemary-infused ghee adds rich flavor and provides the buttery base for the maple syrup and Dijon mustard to marry in. Be sure to use pure maple syrup for the best quality and taste.

INGREDIENTS:

- 2 bone-in pork chops
- 2 Tbsp. ghee, divided
- 10 ounces petite carrots, peeled and halved lengthwise
- 2 tbsp maple syrup
- 2 tbsp Dijon mustard
- 1/2 tsp minced garlic
- 1/2 tsp. sea salt
- 1/4 tsp. black pepper
- 2 small sprigs of rosemary

EQUIPMENT:

- Medium cast iron skillet
- Tongs
- Small bowl

DIRECTIONS:

1 Season pork chops on both sides with sea salt and black pepper. Set aside. Melt 1 tablespoon of ghee in a medium cast iron skillet over medium heat and add carrots. Stir to coat. Cover and cook for 12-15 minutes or until tender. Transfer carrots to a plate.

2 Add remaining tablespoon of ghee to pan over medium heat. When ghee is sizzling, add pork chops and cook for 6 minutes.

3 While pork chops cook stir together maple syrup and Dijon mustard in a small bowl. When the first side has browned, flip pork chops using tongs and add garlic to the pan along with maple-Dijon mixture and rosemary sprigs. Continue to cook for 6 minutes.

4 Return cooked carrots to the pan and spoon maple-Dijon mixture over carrots and pork chops. Continue to cook for 3 minutes longer to warm carrots through.

PORK CHOPS WITH BUTTERY MUSHROOM SAUCE

PREP
5
MINUTES

COOK
27
MINUTES

TOTAL
32
MINUTES

SERVES
4

One-pan meals are a no-fuss way to cook at home without the hassle of cleanup. In this savory recipe, pork chops are seared in butter creating the perfect backdrop for the mushroom sauce. The browned bits from the pan make for a rich and savory gravy without a lot of extra ingredients.

This dish can be served over cauliflower rice to soak up the gravy or alongside your favorite grain-free crusty bread.

INGREDIENTS:

- 4 boneless pork chops
- 2 Tbsp. butter, divided
- 2 cups sliced white button mushrooms
- 4 sprigs fresh thyme
- 2 cloves garlic, minced
- 1/2 cup chicken stock
- 1 tsp. arrowroot powder

- 1/2 tsp. sea salt
- 1/4 tsp. black pepper

EQUIPMENT:

- 10-inch skillet
- Wooden spatula
- Whisk

DIRECTIONS:

1 Melt 1 tablespoon of butter in a medium skillet over medium-high heat for 2 minutes. Blot pork chops dry with paper towel and season with salt and pepper on both sides. Place chops in skillet and brown for 6 minutes on each side. Set pork chops aside on a plate and reduce heat to medium.

2 Melt remaining tablespoon of butter in skillet and scrape up any bits of browned pork using a wooden spatula. Add mushrooms, thyme and garlic. Sauté for 7 minutes or until mushrooms are tender. Remove thyme sprigs and discard. Slowly whisk in arrowroot flour then add chicken stock. Bring to a simmer for 3 minutes to thicken sauce. Add pork chops back to pan and heat through for 2-3 minutes. Serve hot.

SMOTHERED PORK CHOPS WITH SMOKY SWEET POTATO MASH

PREP
10 MINUTES

COOK
10 MINUTES

TOTAL
20 MINUTES

SERVES
4

Sweet and smoky reaches a new level with thick, pan-seared pork chops covered in sweet and spicy apple smother, complemented by more smoke-infused sweet potato. This makes a delicious fall meal, with all the flavors and aromas we associate with the weather getting colder.

INGREDIENTS:

- 4 - 1" thick bone-in, pork chops
- 2 medium apples, halved, cored and thinly sliced
- 1 large onion, thinly sliced
- 3 Tbsp. coconut oil, divided
- 1/4 cup apple cider vinegar
- 3-4 medium sweet potatoes
- 6 cups chicken or vegetable broth
- 1/2 tsp. chipotle chili powder
- 1 tsp. smoked paprika
- Sea salt and fresh cracked pepper, to taste

EQUIPMENT:

- Large skillet
- Medium-sized pot

DIRECTIONS:

1 Use a paper towel to pat dry the pork chops and season each side liberally with salt and pepper. In a large skillet over medium-high heat melt 2 Tbsp. coconut oil and sear the pork chops until they start to brown - approximately 2 minutes each side. Remove from the heat and set aside.

2 In the same skillet add thinly sliced onion and apple slices along with a pinch of salt and pepper, lowering the heat to medium. Sauté for about 5 minutes, stirring occasionally, and then add the vinegar and cook another minute, stirring to scrape all brown bits from bottom of pan.

3 At this time add the chops back to the pan spooning some of the apples and onions on top. Lower the heat to simmer, cover the pan and continue cooking until chops are cooked through and tender.

4 To prepare the potatoes, wash, peel and chop into 1" cubes, and add to a medium-sized pot. Pour in the broth so that the potatoes are just covered with liquid. Cover with a lid and bring to a boil over high heat. Cook until the potatoes are fork tender. Drain all but 1/2 cup of broth, add 1 Tbsp. of coconut oil, paprika, chili powder and sea salt and mash until smooth. Serve sweet potato mash alongside the chops, apples and onions.

INSTANT POT ASIAN BABY BACK RIBS

PREP
10
MINUTES

COOK
33
MINUTES

TOTAL
43
MINUTES

SERVES
2-3

These melt in your mouth baby back ribs have an added zing thanks to the Asian-inspired basting sauce. And with your trusty Instant pot, these can be on the table in less than an hour. Pair with a salad topped with sesame dressing or any vegetable of your choosing for a complete, well-rounded meal!

INGREDIENTS:

- 4 lbs. baby back ribs, membrane removed

For Rub:

- 2 Tbsp. coconut sugar
- 1 tsp. smoked paprika
- 1 tsp. gochujang powder or a few pinches of cayenne pepper
- 1/2 tsp. onion powder
- 1/2 tsp. garlic powder
- 1/2 tsp. ground ginger
- 1 tsp. sea salt

For Basting Sauce:

- 1/4 cup tomato paste
- 3 Tbsp. pineapple juice
- 3 Tbsp. coconut aminos
- 1 Tbsp. raw honey
- 2 tsp. Dijon mustard
- 1/2 tsp. smoked paprika
- 1/8 tsp. cayenne pepper

EQUIPMENT:

- Instant pot/pressure cooker
- Baking sheet

DIRECTIONS:

1 Stir together ingredients for rub. Place ribs on work surface and massage the rub into the meaty side with your hands.

2 Add 1 cup of water to instant pot and place the trivet that came with Instant Pot inside. Fold ribs and place standing up on trivet inside of instant pot.

3 Lock lid and close vent valve. Press Manual setting for 25 minutes. While ribs cook, stir together ingredients for basting sauce.

4 Allow pressure to naturally release before opening vent valve and releasing remaining pressure. Remove ribs from pot and place on a large baking sheet. Liberally coat ribs with sauce.

5 Transfer ribs to middle rack of oven and broil for 6-8 minutes to caramelize sauce. Rest ribs at room temperature for 5-10 minutes before slicing.

SLOW COOKER BBQ PULLED PORK

PREP
10
MINUTES

COOK
8
HOURS

TOTAL
8.25
HOURS

SERVES
4-6

This set-it-and-forget-it recipe is the perfect entrée for busy days or meal prepping. The ingredients are combined in a slow cooker and cooked to tender goodness for easy shredding. A pork roast is the ideal cut of meat because of its size and flavor. Pork roast has a layer of fat on top that adds juicy goodness to the other ingredients while cooking.

You can serve this pulled pork on gluten-free buns or pile it on top of shredded veggies for a barbecue-style Buddha bowl! Looking for sides? Choose one or all of these to serve alongside the pulled pork...

- Dill pickles
- Baked sweet potato fries
- Coleslaw (dairy-free)

INGREDIENTS:

- 48 oz. boneless pork roast
- 2 Tbsp. coconut sugar
- 2 tsp. chili powder
- 1 tsp. smoked paprika
- 1/2 tsp. cumin
- 1/4 tsp. cayenne pepper
- 1/4 tsp. onion powder
- 1 cup unsweetened tomato sauce

- 1/2 cup chicken stock
- 1 Tbsp. pure maple syrup
- 1 tsp. minced garlic
- 1 tsp. sea salt

EQUIPMENT:

- Small mixing bowl
- Slow cooker

DIRECTIONS:

1 Stir together tomato sauce, garlic, chicken stock, and maple syrup in a small bowl. Pour into the bottom of crockpot.

2 Place pork roast on a cutting board and blot dry with paper towel. In a small mixing bowl stir together dry seasonings. Massage 1 tablespoon of dry rub onto the fatty side of pork roast. Stir remaining dry rub into tomato mixture in slow cooker.

3 Place pork roast in slow cooker. Cover and cook 8 hours on medium setting. Shred pork using 2 forks and return to crockpot. Stir well to coat pork in sauce. Serve hot.

SLOW COOKER PORK CARNITAS

PREP
10
MINUTES

COOK
8
HOURS

TOTAL
8.25
HOURS

SERVES
6

CERTIFIED PALEO • **P** • KETO FRIENDLY • **K** • GLUTEN FREE • DAIRY FREE

The crockpot is the perfect set-it-and-forget-it answer for busy days and weekends when spending time in the kitchen isn't an option. In this shredded carnitas recipe the slow cooker does all of the work, slow-cooking pork to fork tender. It's perfect for piling on Paleo tortillas with fresh toppings like pickled onion, tomatoes or fresh cilantro.

INGREDIENTS:

- 3 lb. boneless pork roast
- 1/2 a white onion, thinly sliced
- 1 cup chicken stock
- Juice of 1 lime
- 2 tsp. cumin
- 1 tsp. chili powder
- 1/2 tsp. oregano
- 1/2 tsp. cayenne pepper
- 1 tsp. minced garlic
- 1/2 tsp. sea salt

For Tortillas (optional):

- 1 cup cassava flour
- 1 1/4 cup unsweetened almond milk
- 2 large eggs
- 1/4 tsp. sea salt
- Avocado oil or tallow

EQUIPMENT:

- Slow cooker
- Medium baking pan
- Tongs
- Medium mixing bowl
- Skillet

DIRECTIONS:

1 Combine carnitas ingredients in slow cooker and set temperature to high. Cover and cook for 6-8 hours or until pork shreds easily with a fork.

2 Turn oven to broil. Shred pork and place back into slow cooker to absorb liquid. Use tongs to transfer pork to a medium baking pan. Broil for 5-7 minutes until edges of pork and onion are crisp and browned.

3 Serve carnitas hot over Paleo tortilla or in a bowl with your favorite toppings!

To make the cassava flour tortillas: Stir together ingredients in a medium mixing bowl until smooth and thoroughly combined. Heat a medium skillet over medium heat for 3 minutes and lightly grease with avocado oil or tallow. Pour 1/4 cup of batter into the center of pan and cook for 4-5 minutes. Flip with a spatula and cook an additional 4-5 minutes. Transfer to a plate and repeat with remaining batter.

ORANGE SPICED PORK ROAST WITH HARICOTS VERTS

PREP
15
MINUTES

COOK
2.5
HOURS

TOTAL
3
HOURS

SERVES
3-4

Minimum prep work and a long roasting time means more time for you to sit back and relax before enjoying a juicy, zesty pork roast. Served alongside haricots verts, which are slightly longer, skinnier green beans, make this a delicious, full meal.

INGREDIENTS:

- 1 1/2 lbs. pork roast
- 3 garlic cloves, minced
- 1 tsp. rosemary
- 3 oranges; 1 cut into wedges, 1 juiced and zested, and 1 cut into thin slices
- 3 Tbsp. avocado oil or tallow (divided)
- 1/4 tsp. cardamom
- 1/4 tsp. ground cloves

- 1/4 tsp. ground anise
- 3 cups haricots verts
- 1/2 tsp. salt
- 1/2 tsp. cracked pepper
- Rosemary sprigs for garnish

EQUIPMENT:

- Large skillet
- Oven proof dish

DIRECTIONS:

1 Preheat oven to 450°F. Combine garlic, rosemary, salt and pepper to make a paste. Pierce pork roast with a sharp knife in several places and stuff the piercings with orange slices. Rub 1 tablespoon avocado oil or tallow, paste, and seasonings all over pork loin. Place in an oven-proof dish and roast, uncovered, in the oven for 30 to 45 minutes. Reduce the oven temperature to 350°F and continue cooking an additional 1 hour.

2 Remove roast from oven and add orange juice to the pan, along with a rosemary sprig on top. Cook an additional 1 to 1 1/2 hours, or until the meat shreds easily with a fork. Check often to make sure the orange juice hasn't evaporated entirely. If so, add additional water.

3 When the roast is nearly finished, heat a skillet over medium-high heat. Add 1 teaspoon avocado oil or tallow. Heat for one minute. Add orange slices and sear on each side so they have dark brown edges. Set aside and use as a garnish for the roast.

4 Add 2 teaspoons avocado oil or tallow to the skillet and heat for a minute. Add haricots verts and the rest of the seasonings and cook until browned bits appear, but the haricots are still crisp. Add a little water if needed, so it doesn't burn. Sprinkle with salt, pepper, and orange zest. Remove roast from oven and garnish with orange slices, then serve with haricots verts.

SLOW COOKER CARNITAS WITH FAJITA VEGGIES

PREP
10
MINUTES

COOK
7-8
HOURS

TOTAL
8
HOURS

SERVES
7-8

Whether it's taco Tuesday or fajita Friday, these crockpot carnitas will definitely become a staple in your rotation of Mexican-inspired dishes. Slow cooked for 7-8 hours, start these in the morning for a juicy, fall apart pork shoulder by dinner time. Paired with a dairy-free avocado cream sauce that you can make as spicy as you like by adjusting the amount of jalapeño added.

INGREDIENTS:

- 1 pork shoulder
- Juice from 2 oranges
- Juice from 2 limes
- 2 cups bell peppers of choice, sliced
- 1 large yellow onion, sliced
- 1 Tbsp. maple syrup
- 4 garlic cloves, minced
- 2 bay leaves
- 2 Tbsp. avocado oil or tallow
- 2 tsp. each salt and paprika
- 1 tsp. each of black pepper, garlic powder, onion powder, cumin, and oregano

For Creamy Avocado Sauce:

- 1 ripe avocado
- 1/2 cup cilantro, packed
- 1/2 medium white onion, chopped
- 1 garlic clove, minced
- Juice from 1 lime
- 1/2 – 1 jalapeño, deseeded
- 1/2 tsp. sea salt
- 1/4 cup filtered water

EQUIPMENT:

- Slow cooker
- Food processor or blender

DIRECTIONS:

1 Combine black pepper, garlic powder, onion powder, cumin, oregano, salt and paprika. Evenly coat the pork with the spices.

2 Add bell peppers, onion, orange juice, lime juice, maple syrup, garlic, oil and bay leaves to your slow cooker.

3 Cover the pot and cook on low for 7-8 hours, or until the meat shreds easily.

4 To make the sauce, add all ingredients to a food processor or blender and process until smooth. If too thick, add water by one tablespoon until you reach a desired consistency.

5 Serve roast shredded atop fajita veggies, with avocado sauce spread on top.

SPICY CACAO PULLED PORK

PREP
15
MINUTES

COOK
7
HOURS

TOTAL
7.25
HOURS

SERVES
7-8

This long roasting time will fill your house with sweet cacao aromas that will have everyone's mouths watering! Plus, with only 15 minutes of prep time this is the perfect illusion that you've been working in the kitchen all day when in reality, it's a quick 15 minutes of prep time and that's it!

INGREDIENTS:

- 1 pork shoulder roast
- 4 Tbsp. olive oil (divided)
- 1 1/2 cups vegetable or chicken broth
- 3 cups fresh dandelion or other leafy green
- Sea salt to taste

  For Cacao Spice Rub:

- 2 Tbsp. + 3/4 tsp. ground cinnamon
- 2 Tbsp. coarse sea salt

- 1 Tbsp. + 2 tsp. unsweetened cacao powder
- 1 tsp. ground white peppercorns
- 1 tsp. ground coriander seeds
- 1 tsp. ground nutmeg
- 1/2 tsp. ground cloves

EQUIPMENT:

- Slow cooker
- Sauté pan

DIRECTIONS:

1 Combine spices for cacao rub. Rub pork with 2 tablespoons oil, then follow by coating the roast in the rub.

2 Add roast to the slow cooker with broth. Cover and cook on high for roughly 6-7 hours, or until the meat pulls and separates easily.

3 When the roast is nearly done, add oil to a pan, followed by greens of choice. Sauté until just wilted.

4 Serve the pork roast over the greens, adding sea salt to taste.

HONEY BALSAMIC PORK WITH SPICY CARROTS

PREP
5
MINUTES

COOK
45
MINUTES

TOTAL
50
MINUTES

SERVES
2

This pork is beautifully glazed with a rosemary-honey Balsamic sauce for deliciously sticky pork. This sauce is so good, you'll want to pour it over the carrots, and probably anything else on your plate, too!

INGREDIENTS:

- 2 pork steaks
- 1/4 cup Balsamic vinegar
- 3 Tbsp. olive oil (divided)
- 2 Tbsp. honey
- 1 tsp. chopped fresh rosemary
- 1/4 tsp. red pepper flakes
- 1 lb whole carrots
- 1 tsp. chili powder
- Salt and black pepper to taste

EQUIPMENT:

- Skillet
- Baking pan
- Parchment paper
- Small saucepan

DIRECTIONS:

1 Preheat oven to 400°F. Line a baking pan with parchment paper. Place the carrots in a single layer on the baking pan.

2 In a small bowl, mix together 1 tablespoon of olive oil, chili powder, red pepper flakes, salt and pepper. Toss with the carrots to coat. Place in the oven and bake for 25-35 minutes or until carrots are tender and browned. Time may vary depending on the thickness of the carrots.

3 When the carrots are nearly done, begin cooking the Balsamic vinegar, honey, remaining olive oil, and rosemary in a small saucepan over medium heat until the mixture begins to bubble lightly. Remove from heat.

4 Transfer about 2 tablespoons of the Balsamic glaze to a small bowl and set aside. Season the pork steaks with salt and pepper, then brush with the remaining glaze.

5 Add the pork to the skillet and cook for 4-5 minutes each side, depending on thickness. If you have a thermometer, a medium-done pork steak will read 140°F.

6 Remove the steaks and brush with the reserved glaze (use a clean brush). Serve alongside spicy carrots.

KOREAN PORK WITH ROASTED RADICCHIO

PREP
5
MINUTES

COOK
27
MINUTES

TOTAL
32
MINUTES

SERVES
2

A Korean-inspired recipe is perfect for pork steaks thanks to their lean, mild flavor, making them the perfect vessel for this delicious sauce. It is then paired with radicchio, which is roasted, helping to mellow it's slightly bitter flavor.

INGREDIENTS:

- 2 pork steaks, patted dry
- Sea salt and pepper, to taste
- 1 small radicchio, cut into large disks
- 1 Tbsp. avocado oil

For Sauce:

- 1/2 apple, roughly chopped
- 1/4 cup coconut aminos or gluten-free tamari sauce
- 1 Tbsp. apple cider vinegar
- 1 tsp. fish sauce
- 1/2 Tbsp. avocado oil
- 2 garlic cloves
- 1" fresh ginger

EQUIPMENT:

- Food processor
- Baking sheet
- Parchment paper

DIRECTIONS:

1 Preheat oven to 350°F. Sprinkle meat on both sides with salt, pepper. Chop the radicchio into large disks and drizzle with 1 tablespoon avocado oil.

2 Place both on a parchment-lined baking sheet in one layer and bake for 25 minutes, turning the pork steaks once.

3 While the steaks are baking, prepare the sauce. Place sauce ingredients in a food processor until thick and smooth. Set aside.

4 Remove the steaks and radicchio from oven when done. Brush the steaks with the sauce and place them back in the oven on broil for 2 minutes. Remove and serve, adding an optional extra dash of salt and pepper.

OVEN BARBECUED PORK STEAKS

PREP
10
MINUTES

COOK
60
MINUTES

TOTAL
70
MINUTES

SERVES
4

Smoky barbecue flavor isn't reserved only for outdoor grilling in the summertime. With this simple barbecue pork steak recipe you can achieve the tender, smoky flavor of grilling indoors, complete with delicious, homemade barbecue sauce! But if you're pressed for time, feel free to use your favorite barbecue sauce.

INGREDIENTS:

- 2 pork steaks
- 1/4 tsp. sea salt
- 1/8 tsp. black pepper

  For Barbecue Sauce:
- 1/3 cup tomato paste
- 1/4 cup coconut aminos
- 2 Tbsp. maple syrup
- 1 tsp. ground cumin
- 1 tsp. smoked paprika
- 1/8 tsp. onion powder

EQUIPMENT:

- Medium baking pan
- Parchment paper
- Small mixing bowl
- Tongs

DIRECTIONS:

1 Preheat oven to 350ºF and line a baking sheet with parchment paper. Blot pork steaks dry and place on baking sheet. Sprinkle with salt and pepper. Mix together ingredients for barbecue sauce and reserve half of sauce in a small bowl for serving.

2 Spread half of remaining barbecue sauce over pork steaks, tent with parchment paper. Bake for 30 minutes. Carefully remove parchment paper and flip steaks using tongs. Increase oven temperature to 400ºF. Pour remaining sauce on top. Return to oven for 25-30 minutes longer, uncovered. Remove from oven and rest pork steaks at room temperature for 5 minutes before slicing. Serve hot with reserved sauce.

OVEN 'FRIED' PORK STEAKS

PREP
10
MINUTES

COOK
40
MINUTES

TOTAL
50
MINUTES

SERVES
2-4

Also known as a Boston butt or pork blade, pork steaks are cut from the shoulder of the pig and are known for having lean, tender meat. With this recipe, the pork is coated in almond meal to add a delicious crunch to an otherwise tender cut of pork.

INGREDIENTS:

- 2-4 pork steaks
- 1 egg
- 1 1/2 cups almond meal
- 2 cups fresh green beans
- 1 cup diced sweet potato
- 1 Tbsp. olive or avocado oil
- 2 Tbsp. Dijon mustard
- 1 tsp. dried rosemary

- 1/2 tsp. dried basil
- 1/8 tsp. garlic powder
- 1/2 tsp. salt
- 1/8 tsp. ground black pepper

EQUIPMENT:

- Baking pan
- Small bowl for mixing

DIRECTIONS:

1 Preheat oven to 375°F. Whisk the egg in a small bowl. Combine the almond meal with seasonings and place on a plate. Blot the pork steaks dry with a paper towel, brush on a light layer of Dijon, then dip into the egg. Let any excess liquid drip off and dredge in the almond meal mixture, coating all sides. Place the pork steaks onto the baking pan.

2 Coat green beans and diced sweet potato in olive or avocado oil and a dash of sea salt, and arrange around the pork steaks. Bake for 30 minutes. Flip the steaks, then return to the oven.

3 Cook for 10 more minutes or until golden brown. Serve garnished with fresh herbs.

SPICY KALUA PORK STEAKS

PREP
30
MINUTES

MARINADE
30
MINUTES

COOK
2
HOURS

TOTAL
2.5
HOURS

SERVES
2

This generally hands-off crockpot recipe makes for an amazing Hawaiian-inspired dish that will transport you to the islands. Marinated in orange juice and then cooked alongside pineapple and onions in the slow cooker, these pork steaks turn out juicy, sweet, and loaded with flavor.

INGREDIENTS:

- 2 pork steaks
- 1 orange, juiced
- 1 pineapple, cut and diced into chunks, or two small cans of pineapple chunks
- 1 medium onion, chopped
- 1 Tbsp. olive oil
- 1/4 cup water
- 1 tsp. chili flakes
- 2 tsp. paprika (divided)

EQUIPMENT:

- Slow cooker
- Bowl or bag

DIRECTIONS:

1 Begin by combining orange juice and pork steaks in a bowl or bag, and letting marinade for 30 minutes.

2 Once marinated, toss pineapple chunks with sliced onion and 1 teaspoon paprika. Add to the bottom of your slow cooker.

3 Discard the orange juice and brush each pork steak with olive oil and the other teaspoon of paprika. Arrange with the pineapple in the slow cooker.

4 Add the water to the cooker, followed by a sprinkling of the chili flakes to top everything.

5 Cover and cook for 2 hours. Serve with salt and pepper to taste.

WILD-CAUGHT SEAFOOD

FRESH FROM THEIR NATURAL HABITAT

Unlike the farm-raised that you'll find in your local grocery store, wild-caught seafood eat a natural diet and are free to move about the ocean. In contrast, farm-raised fish are kept in small, crowded areas and often treated with antibiotics to prevent the spread of infection. They also have up to 20% less protein than wild-raised seafood, and contain higher levels of inflammation causing omega-6 fatty acids.

Buying wild-caught seafood is a no brainer. It tastes better, it's better for you, and more sustainable. At Wild Pastures we have found some of the highest-quality seafood raised in the USA by wild-caught farmers and are ready to deliver it right to your doorstep.

CARIBBEAN SHRIMP SALAD

PREP
10
MINUTES

COOK
6
MINUTES

TOTAL
75
MINUTES

SERVES
2

This refreshing Caribbean shrimp salad is full of island flavor with crunchy jicama and juicy mango! Steamed shrimp is tossed in a tangy-smoky blend of seasoning before serving alongside the vibrant fruit and vegetables. This salad is high in free-radical fighting antioxidants and will fill you up without weighing you down!

INGREDIENTS:

- 1/2 lb. large shrimp, peeled/deveined
- 1 Tbsp. lime juice
- 1/2 tsp. lime zest
- 1/4 tsp. sea salt
- 1/8 tsp. paprika
- 1/8 tsp. dried thyme
- 1/8 tsp. onion powder
- Pinch of cayenne pepper

For Salad:

- 1 cup shredded leafy lettuce
- 1/2 cup thinly sliced mango
- 1/2 cup halved cherry tomatoes
- 1/2 cup peeled/chopped baby cucumber

- 1/4 cup peeled or chopped jicama
- 2 Tbsp. chopped red onion
- 2 Tbsp. chopped cilantro
- 3-4 thin slices of jalapeño
- 2 Tbsp. olive oil
- 1/4 tsp. sea salt
- 2 lime wedges

EQUIPMENT:

- Steaming basket (optional)
- Large pot
- Mixing bowl

DIRECTIONS:

1 Steam shrimp on stovetop or boil in 1 quart of water until pink, 5-6 minutes. Strain and chill until cold, about 1 hour.

2 Add shrimp to a medium mixing bowl and add lime juice, lime zest, sea salt, thyme, onion powder, paprika and cayenne pepper. Stir to coat shrimp.

3 Assemble shrimp, red onion, cucumber, tomatoes, mango, jicama and lettuce in a serving bowl. Top with sliced jalapeño, cilantro and sea salt. Drizzle olive oil over top and squeeze lime on vegetables. Enjoy right away.

COLLARD GREEN SHRIMP ROLLS

PREP
15
MINUTES

COOK
8
MINUTES

TOTAL
1.5
HOURS

SERVES
2

These light and refreshing shrimp roll-ups are the perfect snack or lunch for warmer months. Each collard green is filled with antioxidant-rich raw veggies and steamed shrimp complete with a creamy avocado dipping sauce that gets its texture from avocado instead of dairy!

INGREDIENTS:

- 1/4 lb. shrimp peeled/ deveined/tails removed
- 4 large collard green leaves
- 1 baby cucumber, julienned
- 1/2 cup shredded purple cabbage
- 1/2 cup matchstick carrots
- 1/3 cup cilantro (divided)

  For Avocado-Cilantro Dipping Sauce:

- 1/2 a ripe medium avocado, peeled
- 1/3 cup fresh lime juice

- 1/4 cup filtered water
- 2 Tbsp. raw honey
- Small handful of cilantro
- 1 clove garlic
- 1 tsp sea salt

EQUIPMENT:

- Steamer (optional)
- Food processor/blender
- Large pot

DIRECTIONS:

1 Steam shrimp or boil in 1 quart of boiling water until pink, about 5-6 minutes. Strain and chill in refrigerator for 1 hour.

2 Combine ingredients for dipping sauce in a food processor or blender and blend until smooth. Transfer to a small jar.

3 Bring 6 cups of water to a boil over medium high heat in a large pot. Add 2 collard green leaves and cook for 1-2 minutes. Place collard green leaves on a paper towel-lined plate and repeat with remaining leaves.

4 Blot excess moisture from collard greens and slice off the thick center rib. Set leaf on work surface with the stem/rib end facing you. Assemble matchstick carrots, cucumber and cabbage on each leaf with 2 pieces of shrimp. Fold the bottom of the leaf away from you toward the center and fold in the sides. Roll and place on a plate with the seam facing down. Repeat with remaining collard greens.

5 Slice rolls in half and serve right away with dipping sauce or refrigerate up to 24 hours.

SESAME SALMON WITH CARROT GINGER SLAW

PREP
15
MINUTES

COOK
15
MINUTES

TOTAL
30
MINUTES

SERVES
4

This Asian-inspired sesame salmon is served over a vibrant slaw that is full of healthy ingredients like purple cabbage, fresh ginger and avocado oil. Salmon is roasted in an aromatic combination of toasted sesame oil and garlic with sweet raw honey and coconut aminos adding depth. Although the salmon is roasted, it is equally delicious chilled for 2 hours and served alongside the slaw in warmer months.

INGREDIENTS:

- 1 lb. salmon filet

  For Marinade:

- 1/4 cup coconut aminos
- 2 Tbsp. toasted sesame oil
- 2 Tbsp. fresh lime juice
- 1 Tbsp. raw honey
- 1 tsp. minced garlic
- 1/2 tsp. sea salt

  For Carrot Ginger Slaw:

- 4 cups shredded or matchstick carrots
- 1 cup shredded purple cabbage

- 1/4 cup chopped cilantro
- 2 Persian cucumbers, lightly peeled and sliced into half moons
- 2 Tbsp. avocado oil
- 2 Tbsp. fresh lime juice
- 1 Tbsp. raw honey
- 2 tsp. grated ginger
- 1/2 tsp. sea salt
- 2 tsp. toasted sesame seeds

EQUIPMENT:

- Baking sheet
- Parchment paper

DIRECTIONS:

1 Preheat oven to 425°F and lightly grease a baking sheet with parchment paper. Position oven rack to 1 spot below the top. Pat salmon dry and place in a shallow dish. Whisk together marinade until honey is thoroughly incorporated. Pour over salmon and marinate for 5 minutes.

2 Transfer salmon to baking sheet and roast for 10 minutes. Turn the oven to broil and broil 3-5 minutes longer to lightly char salmon.

3 While salmon roasts, combine carrots, cabbage, cucumber, cilantro and ginger in a medium mixing bowl. Stir together avocado oil, lime juice, honey, sea salt in a small bowl and pour over slaw. Toss to coat. Top with toasted sesame seeds.

4 Serve warm salmon over slaw topped with additional cilantro and sesame seeds.

APRICOT GLAZED SALMON + PISTACHIO BASIL CAULIFLOWER RICE

PREP
10
MINUTES

COOK
30
MINUTES

TOTAL
40
MINUTES

SERVES
4

This sweet and tangy apricot glazed salmon cooks up in just 30 minutes with a crunchy pistachio-basil rice. This dish is perfect for summer or well into fall with its hearty texture and rich flavors. If you don't have apricot preserves, peach is also delicious.

INGREDIENTS:

- 4 salmon filets (5-6 oz each)

  For Apricot Glaze:

- 1/4 cup apricot preserves
- 1 Tbsp. Balsamic vinegar
- 1 garlic clove, minced
- 1/2 tsp. sea salt
- 1/8 tsp. cracked black pepper

  For Pistachio Basil Cauliflower Rice:

- 4 cups riced cauliflower

- 2 Tbsp. olive oil
- 1/4 cup chopped pistachios
- 1/2 cup chopped basil
- 1/4 tsp. dried thyme
- 2 Tbsp. fresh lemon juice
- 1 tsp. sea salt

EQUIPMENT:

- Baking sheet
- Medium mixing bowl

DIRECTIONS:

1 Preheat oven to 400°F. Spread riced cauliflower on a baking sheet and drizzle with olive oil. Use a spatula to stir and coat with oil. Bake for 15 minutes, stirring after 10 minutes. Remove from oven and transfer to a medium mixing bowl. Cool while cooking salmon.

2 Blot surface of salmon dry with paper towel. Stir together ingredients for apricot glaze and spread onto salmon evenly. Bake salmon on a baking sheet for 15 minutes or until fully cooked.

3 Stir lemon juice, pistachios, basil, thyme and sea salt into cauliflower rice. Serve salmon with rice.

GRILLED ENDIVE + SALMON SALAD

PREP
10
MINUTES

COOK
15
MINUTES

TOTAL
35
MINUTES

SERVES
4

Grilled salmon and crunchy endive take on a smoky flavor perfect for summer grilling. Once grilled, the salad comes together with cherry tomatoes, heart-healthy walnuts and a tangy lemon-herb vinaigrette. This recipe is high in protein, healthy fats and antioxidants making it a complete meal on its own.

INGREDIENTS:

- 1 lb. wild-caught salmon filets

For Marinade:

- 1/4 cup lemon juice
- 1 Tbsp. raw honey
- 1 tsp. minced garlic
- 1 tsp. dried basil
- 1/2 tsp. sea salt
- 1/4 tsp. cracked black pepper
- 1 1/2 Tbsp. avocado oil (divided)

For Salad:

- 6 endive leaves, halved lengthwise
- 1 Tbsp. avocado oil, divided
- 1 cup cherry tomatoes, halved
- 1/2 red onion, diced
- 1/2 cup raw walnuts, coarsely chopped
- 1/2 cup chopped parsley

For Vinaigrette:

- 1 lemon, juiced and zested
- 1 clove garlic
- 1/2 tsp. dried oregano
- 1/4 cup avocado oil
- Pinch of salt and pepper

EQUIPMENT:

- Food processor/blender
- Grill or cast iron grill pan

DIRECTIONS:

1 Combine ingredients for salad dressing in a blender or food processor and blend for 30 seconds. Transfer to a small jar and refrigerate until serving.

2 Marinate salmon filets in lemon juice, avocado oil, garlic, basil, honey, sea salt and black pepper for 10 minutes.

3 Heat a cast iron skillet over medium-high heat and grease with avocado oil. Heat pan for 3 minutes. Place salmon on pan, skin side up and cook for 5 minutes. Turn salmon and cover with lid. Cook 4 minutes longer or until flesh is opaque. Set aside on a plate.

4 Grease a cast iron grill pan with 1/2 tablespoon of avocado oil. Brush remaining oil on endive. Place endive on grill pan, cut side down. Grill for 2 minutes. Remove and place on serving plate.

5 Top grilled endive with salmon, cherry tomatoes, red onion, walnuts and parsley. Drizzle with vinaigrette and serve right away.

PECAN CRUSTED SALMON PATTIES

PREP
15
MINUTES

COOK
20
MINUTES

TOTAL
35
MINUTES

SERVES
4

These Paleo salmon patties are pecan crusted for nutty flavor, toasting as they pan fry. Herbs like dill and parsley add a pop of freshness. Baked salmon adds a dose of heart-healthy, fatty acids and ample protein to keep you feeling full.

INGREDIENTS:

- 1 lb. salmon fillet
- 1 cup finely chopped raw pecans
- 1/2 cup finely chopped red bell pepper
- 2 Tbsp. chopped fresh dill
- 1/4 cup finely chopped parsley
- 1 large egg + 1 egg white
- 1 tsp. minced garlic
- 1 tsp. sea salt
- 1/2 tsp. cracked black pepper
- 2 Tbsp. avocado oil

For Sauce:

- 1/2 cup Paleo-friendly mayonnaise
- 2 Tbsp. fresh lemon juice
- 2 tsp. Dijon mustard

EQUIPMENT:

- Sauté pan
- Baking sheet
- Parchment paper
- Medium mixing bowl

DIRECTIONS:

1 Preheat oven to 375°F. Rinse and pat dry the salmon fillet. Line sheet pan with parchment paper and bake for approximately 12-15 minutes, or until the flesh flakes easily with a fork. Remove from the oven and allow to cool completely.

2 While salmon is cooling, stir together ingredients for sauce in a small bowl.

3 Flake salmon using a fork and discard skin. Add to a medium mixing bowl along with the egg, bell pepper, garlic, parsley, dill, sea salt and black pepper. Stir well.

4 Form mixture into patties, coat with pecans and sauté in avocado oil until lightly browned on both sides, about 3 minutes per side.

5 Serve on a bed of greens topped with sauce.

SEARED SCALLOPS WITH CAPER BUTTER SAUCE

PREP
15
MINUTES

COOK
11
MINUTES

TOTAL
26
MINUTES

SERVES
2-3

For a coastal inspired dish, these quick and easy seared scallops are a one-pan wonder! Pillowy jumbo scallops are pan seared in olive oil until golden brown on both sides adding rich flavor. Butter, garlic, capers and fresh lemon juice are added to the pan creating a tangy sauce with depth thanks to the caramelized bits from searing the scallops.

INGREDIENTS:

- 1 lb. jumbo scallops, thawed if frozen
- 2 Tbsp. olive oil
- 1/4 cup unsalted grass fed butter
- 2 Tbsp. lemon juice
- 2 Tbsp. capers
- 2 cloves garlic, minced
- 1/2 tsp. sea salt
- 1/8 tsp. cracked black pepper
- 1/4 cup chopped parsley

EQUIPMENT:

- Cast iron skillet

DIRECTIONS:

1 Blot scallops dry with paper towel to remove surface moisture and season with sea salt and black pepper. Let scallops sit at room temperature for 10 minutes.

2 Heat olive oil in a large cast iron skillet over medium-high heat until shimmering. Add scallops and sear for 3-4 minutes on each side. Set scallops aside on a plate and reduce heat to medium-low.

3 Add butter and garlic to pan and cook 1 minute until butter is melted and bubbling. Stir in lemon juice and capers. Return scallops to pan and cook 2 minutes longer. Serve hot topped with chopped parsley.

LEMON GARLIC BAKED COD WITH FRESH HERBS

PREP
5
MINUTES

COOK
20
MINUTES

TOTAL
25
MINUTES

SERVES
2

Cod is the perfect white fish for oven baking, because it has a much meatier texture than many other white fish like tilapia and a much healthier nutrient profile. It is loaded with immune boosting vitamin D and is a milder alternative to salmon. The buttery lemon sauce seals in a rich flavor that is synonymous with seafood while still keeping the recipe paleo. Serve alongside sautéed asparagus, roasted Brussels sprouts or mashed cauliflower for a complete meal.

INGREDIENTS:

- 1 lb. cod, sliced into 4 pieces
- 1 lemon, sliced into thin wheels
- 2 Tbsp. chopped parsley
- 1 Tbsp. minced chives

  For Sauce:
- 4 Tbsp. unsalted butter
- 1 Tbsp. olive oil
- 1 tsp. minced garlic

- 1/2 tsp. lemon zest
- 1/4 tsp. paprika
- 1/2 tsp. sea salt
- Pinch of cracked black pepper

EQUIPMENT:

- 9x11 baking pan
- Small bowl

DIRECTIONS:

1 Preheat oven to 400°F. Spread sliced lemon on bottom of a 9x11 baking pan. Blot cod with paper towel until dry and place on top of lemon slices.

2 Stir together ingredients for sauce in a small bowl and drizzle on top of cod. Bake for 15 minutes. Turn oven to broil and broil for 4-5 minutes, until cod easily flakes and the top of fish is golden brown.

3 Serve hot topped with chopped parsley and chives.